8-21-72

THE ENGLISH
CEREMONIAL BOOK

THE ENGLISH CEREMONIAL BOOK

A History of Robes, Insignia and
Ceremonies still in use in England

Roger Milton
Line Illustrations by PHILIP MUGFORD

Drake Publishers Inc New York

ISBN 87749-227-1
LoC 71-188803

Published in 1972 by
Drake Publishers Inc
381 Park Avenue South
New York, N.Y. 10016

Printed in Great Britain

1709126

CONTENTS

LIST OF ILLUSTRATIONS

INTRODUCTION

The English Ceremonial Book lays no claim to be a work of scholarship. No new light has been shed on the historical origins of the matters with which it is concerned, and every fact stated may be checked from official records and the writings of learned scholars. What has been attempted is the production for the first time in one volume of an illustrated history of the origins and development to the present day of English ceremonial robes, regalia and insignia still officially in use. And because the trappings by themselves must be meaningless, an attempt has also been made to describe and trace the origins of the ceremonies they adorn. The inclusion of a chapter on the history of the office of herald and of the College of Arms, may be more fully appreciated when it is remembered that only the continuing work of generations of heralds has ensured the survival of so much of the ceremonial of England.

No attempt has been made to include a history of Scottish or Irish ceremonial. It was felt that not only would such an undertaking make the work far too large, but that in the case of Scotland, the Court of the Lord Lyon King of Arms, which controls all Scottish heraldry and ceremonial, had such a different origin and has evolved along such different lines that it deserves a separate volume as befits what was until 1707 a separate kingdom. In the case of Ireland, since 1922 the Republican government has entirely taken over the work of the former Dublin King of Arms; while in Northern Ireland the office of Ulster King of Arms is nowadays attached to that of Norroy King of Arms of England.

Today, thanks to television and the cinema screen, English ceremonial occasions are witnessed and enjoyed by audiences of unprecedented size. To some, their outward appeal will be largely emotional—an emotion based on simple delight in something that is beautiful both in contrasts of colour and in disciplined order of ritual. But will there not also be other thoughts in many people's minds? How did such a ceremony come into existence in the first place? Why do certain officials taking part wear robes or uniforms of a particular shape, colour and style? Why do they carry or wear certain ornaments? To attempt to answer these questions is the purpose of this volume. It is not, though, the only purpose; for the author believes there exists a more profound reason than emotion or curiosity for the enormous public interest—not confined to Britain—in English official pageantry, and that this deeper reason springs from a peculiar quality of the human mind, that it cannot help but look back to the past as well as forward to the future.

That great historian, G. M. Trevelyan, has written that what really distinguishes a civilised nation from one of savages is that the civilised nation possesses a recorded history. It follows, first, that in any age human society is what it is because of the mistakes as well as the successes of its past generations. Secondly, that among civilised people there can be no such thing as a static society. Men and their institutions are continuously changing into something else. But if history teaches anything, it is that too violent an attempt to effect a radical change in political institutions in order to improve social conditions nearly always results in a situation markedly worse than that which the reformers hoped to change, and that these worsened conditions endure for a long time. It has been the proud boast of past generations of Englishmen that their political constitution provided a sure shield to save them in times of change from the worst excesses of revolution that have overtaken so many other countries. The pressures of this day and age, however, are so great that many people, particularly young people with the idealism of their generation, have lost confidence in the working of the British constitution, and the great danger is that the apathy of the majority may leave the way open for an impatient and potentially violent minority to trigger off an explosion that could destroy the work of centuries. It can be no part of this book to offer political solutions to problems which do not lie within its terms of reference. What the author hopes to do is to make ordinary people more aware of what he believes to be true—that the exterior solemnity attending so many of our institutions has a real bearing on these problems, and in a unique way underlines the importance of preserving what has taken so much courage and so much patience to build up over the centuries. Two examples may help to make this clear.

When the Queen drives in state to open Parliament, the ceremonial surrounding the occasion is not there to feed the vanity of monarchs or nobles, but to do honour to a solemn assembly of the Estates of the

Realm. The monarch sitting crowned and robed on the throne, attended by heralds and great officers of state, is not, and never has been in England, the oriental despot demanding the adulation of uncritical flatterers. Even when the Estates were content that the monarch should himself exercise executive power, it was always recognised that that power was allowed by general consent rather than imposed from above. Today, the Queen delegates the executive powers of the Crown to ministers responsible to the people through their elected representatives in Parliament. But she is still the monarch and the ultimate repository of all political function and power. Governments come and governments go; but each government has in its term derived such authority as it has had from the latest of a long line of monarchs whose most important function has always been to represent the continuity of British institutions. 'The King is dead. Long live the King!' is only another way of saying that those good things which have been achieved by past generations will not lightly be thrown away by the present. The Parliament house with robed lords and subfusc Commons attending their Sovereign adorned with the ancient symbols of royalty clearly speaks not of the might of monarchs, but of the majesty of the Estates; just as the sight of the Prime Minister and the Leader of Her Majesty's Opposition, standing side by side behind the Speaker, symbolises the political education of a nation that no longer executes or imprisons those who do not agree with official policy.

The ceremonial attending the opening of county assizes is sometimes attacked on the grounds of being irrelevant to modern times. It is pointed out that the administration of justice would be equally effective at the hands of experienced judges and lawyers wearing lounge suits. There may be some truth in this; but there is also truth in the legal adage that justice should not only be done, but should be seen to be done. The fanfares and stately procession of high sheriff, mayor and aldermen to greet the arrival of My Lords the Queen's Justices clothed in the magnificence of their scarlet and ermine cannot but impress the watching citizenry with the importance and the majesty of the law. It is true that the pageantry surrounding these occasions has evolved from as far back as the age of Norman and early Plantagenet kings who were anxious to impress on unruly barons the supremacy of royal justice. It is also true that until the passing of the Act of Settlement in 1702 the judges were, quite literally, the servants of the King who could dismiss them at his pleasure. But there is little evidence to prove that prior to 1702 the judges were corrupt, and since the separation of the executive and judicial powers of the Crown brought about by that famous Act, the absolute impartiality of Her Majesty's judges has not seriously been questioned. This in contrast to foreign systems that allow loopholes, dictatorships where the judiciary is frankly subordinate to the executive, and systems in which the person of the presiding judge is accorded neither the visual not actual respect commensurate with his office. Today, the encroachment of executive government on the liberties of the subject, though no doubt sometimes necessary in the light of the vastly more complicated society in which modern man lives, makes the impregnability of the common law and its administration even more important. The visible signs of respect for that law and for its administration so clearly demonstrated by the ceremony surrounding English judges and their courts surely plays a not inconsiderable part in preserving public confidence.

The author does not delude himself by thinking that the arguments and opinions he has set forth will command assent from all or even most of his readers. Neither is he prepared to believe that sympathy with his views is confined to the elderly survivors of a more settled generation, any more than he is prepared to believe that violence and iconoclasm are characteristic of more than the fringe of the vast army of modern students and young people generally. The pages that follow are addressed to all those who are honest enough to admit that they enjoy a good show, even though they may have honest reasons for thinking such things unnecessary. They are addressed also to that not inconsiderable body of officials who, in one capacity or another, are called upon to take an active part in these shows. It is possible that many of these latter often resent the inconvenience, if not actual discomfort, of having to make themselves on occasion spectacles for others to gaze upon. It is the sincere hope of author and illustrator that many such, after reading this book, will come to accept that they are indeed performing a most valuable service to the whole community, and that that community itself will learn to value even more and perhaps for a better reason the ancient pageantry of England.

It remains to express the author and illustrator's indebtedness to the many eminent authorities without whose help the compilation of this work would not have been possible. A full list of authorities consulted personally, as well as a list of the more important books and records studied, is given on another page. Three of these eminent authorities have gone out of their way to offer most valuable advice, and criticism. These are Sir Anthony Wagner, KCVO, D.Litt, Garter

King of Arms, who has also given permission to quote from his authoritative work, *History of the Heralds of England*; Major-General P. B. Gillett, CB, OBE, Secretary of the Central Chancery of the Orders of Knighthood, and the directors of Ede & Ravenscroft Ltd, official robe-makers, of Chancery Lane, who have kindly allowed sketches to be made of the valuable robes of peerage and knighthood in their collection.

ROGER MILTON

Chiddingfold, Surrey, 1971.

PROLOGUE

King George VI died suddenly on 6 February 1952. On a cold and foggy morning two days later we walked to St James's Palace, thrusting our way with difficulty through the hurrying crowds of drab citizenry intent on their ordinary pursuits. London in those days had not recovered from the effects of nearly six years' total war; most of the buildings were sooty and badly in need of a coat of paint, and many still bore the chips and gashes the bomb blasts had brought. The police had diverted all traffic from the palace approaches, but there was a large crowd jostling good-humouredly to find a vantage point for what was to follow. Fortunately, we had special passes and were able to squeeze our way through to a privileged position facing the Friary Court. This yard, open on one side to the normally busy street leading to the Mall and St James's Park, is flanked on the other three by the old red-brick walls of the palace which has stood there since Tudor times. In the middle ages a monastery had occupied the site, but following the destruction by fire of the old palace of Westminster, Henry VIII, who had his own ideas about monastic property, converted St James into a new home for himself. It is true that this monarch and most of his Tudor and Stuart successors preferred to spend the greater part of their time in Wolsey's old London residence, now renamed Whitehall, but after this palace was burnt down in 1698 St James's remained the official home of the kings and queens of England and the focal point of royal government, even after George III had transferred himself and his large family to Buckingham House over sixty years later. Ambassadors are accredited to the Court of St James, and since the sixteenth century new monarchs have been first proclaimed from its balcony. It was at this balcony, running the whole length of the palace at the rear of the courtyard, that the assembled citizens were now gazing. Silent and motionless in the courtyard below was a guard of honour and regimental band in the grey greatcoats and tall black bearskins of the Brigade of Guards.

The mellow chimes of the old palace clock struck eleven, and as the last stroke died on the frosty February air one of the tall windows opened, and on to that rather grimy balcony erupted a riot of colour. Blue, green, scarlet and gold—in gorgeous medieval tabards quartered with the royal arms of Britain came the heralds of England: the Kings of Arms, Garter, Clarenceux and Norroy; Lancaster, Windsor, Richmond and other heralds; and Rouge Croix, Blue Mantle, Rouge Dragon and Portcullis, pursuivants. Last of all came Bernard Marmaduke, 16th Duke of Norfolk, Earl Marshal of England, in scarlet and gold levée dress and plumed cocked hat. The Earl Marshal raised his baton, and at either end of the balcony the state trumpeters shattered the still air with a fanfare. Garter King of Arms stepped forward unrolling the parchment proclamation:

' . . . We, therefore, the Lords Spiritual and Temporal, Members of His late Majesty's Most Honourable Privy Council, the Lord Mayor of London, together with other principal gentlemen of quality, with one heart and voice do publish and proclaim that the high and mighty princess Elizabeth Alexandra Mary is now become our Sovereign Liege Lady ELIZABETH II, by the Grace of God Queen of Great Britain and Northern Ireland and of all her other Realms and Territories, Defender of the Faith . . .'

The proclamation ended. The King of Arms lifted his plumed hat high in the air and cried: 'GOD SAVE THE QUEEN!' As the Earl Marshal and the other heralds with hats on high repeated the prayer, the trumpets sounded once more. Then the guard of honour in the court-yard below presented arms and the drums of the band began the long roll preceding the anthem. And so the brief ceremony came to its end. To the distant thunder of a salute of guns from Hyde Park and the joyful pealing of the bells of Westminster, the heralds slowly filed back into the palace. Soon, with an escort of Household Cavalry, they would go through the streets in open carriages to make proclamation again at Charing Cross, at Temple Bar, and lastly in the heart of the City from the steps of the Royal Exchange.

St James's balcony and Friary Court were once more empty and desolate, perhaps to remain so for half a century. Very soon the taxis and cars, the hurrying pedestrians, would take control again, sparing only a casual glance for the empty courtyard and shuttered windows. But for one brief moment of time the curtain had been lifted. Of the thousands who had witnessed this ancient ceremony attending the accession of the latest in a long line of princes to the throne and crown of her ancestors, there can have been very few who had remained unmoved. It might be difficult to say why. There must have been sadness at the remembrance of departed glories—the golden age of the first Elizabeth, the age of Nelson and Wellington, the long Victorian peace, the Empire on which the sun never set. But as well as sadness there was hope, and assurance; a deep-felt feeling that although the old order must always change bringing no one knows what frightening novelties, the golden thread of monarchy would in England continue to link the best of the past with the best of the future. We walked away from Henry VIII's old palace, hurrying to keep out the February cold; but there was a glow in our hearts.

THE COLLEGE OF ARMS
Incorporated by Royal Charters of Richard III, 1483/84, and of Mary I and Philip, 1555

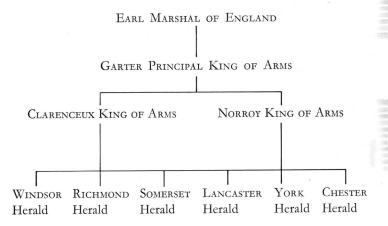

EARL MARSHAL OF ENGLAND

GARTER PRINCIPAL KING OF ARMS

CLARENCEUX KING OF ARMS   NORROY KING OF ARMS

WINDSOR   RICHMOND   SOMERSET   LANCASTER   YORK   CHESTER
Herald   Herald   Herald   Herald   Herald   Herald

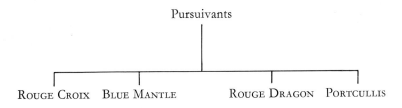

Pursuivants

ROUGE CROIX   BLUE MANTLE   ROUGE DRAGON   PORTCULLIS

NOTE: **The Earl Marshal,** who presides over the College of Arms and the Court of Chivalry, is also responsible for all state ceremony in England. He is advised professionally by the Kings of Arms. Since the seventeenth century, this office has been hereditary in the family of the FitzAllen Dukes of Norfolk.

Garter King of Arms has sovereign rights over the other heralds in their college. He is also the King of Arms of the Order of the Garter and responsible for the genealogies of the Knights Companion.

Clarenceux King of Arms is responsible for all grants of arms and matters of heraldry south of the river Trent. His colleagues are Windsor, Richmond and Somerset Heralds.

Norroy King of Arms has a like responsibility north of the river Trent. His colleagues are Lancaster, York and Chester Heralds.

(In practice, the six heralds are not confined in their duties to one province.)

The four **Pursuivants** (pronounced 'Persevant') are the assistant heralds. They may take their titles from, respectively, Cross of St George, Mantle of the Garter, Dragon of Wales, and the Somerset-Beaufort arms, from which family Henry VII was descended.

1 THE HERALDS AND THE COLLEGE OF ARMS

The Prologue was an attempt to describe what is the rarest and perhaps the most splendid of the many duties the heralds are nowadays called on to perform. They have also the ordering of all state ceremonial; coronations, the opening of parliaments, state funerals, and so forth. At such functions in their medieval tabards they make a not inconsiderable contribution to the brilliance of the scene they are largely responsible for creating. In the following pages an attempt will be made to show how the heralds came to be associated not only with state ceremonial, but with what they themselves might consider the more important part of their work—the recording and granting of arms.

1 : Origins and History of the Heralds

It is not known precisely how the office of herald originated, but it seems likely that in the early middle ages it was equated with that of minstrel in the noble household. The more important feudal nobles employed such officials to arrange entertainments in the great halls of their castles during the long winter nights, and to organise pageants and special ceremonies for the visit of the King or other important persons. As late as the middle of the fourteenth century many of the functions of minstrel and herald were interchangeable, but there can be little doubt that it was the development of the military tournament that brought the heralds into the light of day as a distinct class of official. When a tournament was arranged it was the heralds who were sent out to proclaim it. Nor did their duties end there: they accompanied knights to the field; they announced each challenger by name; and they proclaimed the victors. When points were awarded they kept the score; and they acted as umpires over the observance of rules on which they were expected to be experts.

During most of the twelfth and thirteenth centuries tournaments were under the ban of the Church, but this does not seem to have stopped them altogether. In the latter half of the thirteenth century great tournaments were held in England under the powerful patronage of Edward I, and it is in this warrior king's reign that we first hear of kings of arms, although they were then called 'kings of heralds'. King Edward's Statute of Arms of 1292 which, at the request of the feudal nobility and knights, laid down new laws for the conduct of tournaments, included a direction that neither kings of heralds nor 'minstrels' should carry hidden arms, nor any arms except pointless swords. Only they were directed to wear their 'coats of arms'.

The kings of heralds were attached to the household of the King or royal duke, but these were not the only heralds. All through the middle ages many lords had their own heralds who, from at least the middle of the fourteenth century, took their names from the castle or lordship to which they were attached. The earliest name that has come down to us is Carlisle Herald, who brought the news to Edward III at Westminster that a state of war existed between the vassals of the Kings of England and France in Gascony. This was in April 1338 and marked the beginning of the Hundred Years War. Froissart tells us that a few years earlier Carlisle Herald had been given his title by the King on his expedition against the Scots. Later in this century we hear of other heralds by name: Lancaster, Arundel and Chandos Heralds. These were the personal heralds of, respectively, the Duke of Lancaster, the Earl of Arundel, and Sir John Chandos, who was a founder Knight of the Garter and comrade of the Black Prince.

The semi-royal status and practical independence of the greater feudal barons in their own domains during much of the middle ages greatly enhanced the status of their heralds, who were used to carry out various missions. At the same time the king's heralds were undertaking special duties, such as carrying messages in time of war between kings and princes, and after actual battles recording the number of slain and taken prisoner. At other times they were sent abroad on diplomatic missions, and continued to be employed in the field of diplomacy as late as the first half of the sixteenth century by the Tudor monarchs. By that time most of the great feudal barons had either been slain in the many battles of the Wars of the Roses or, having survived, had lost their independent power to the new-style Renaissance kings. Consequently, the most important reason for great lords maintaining their own heralds no longer existed, and it is no coincidence that a royal charter of Richard III, on the very threshold of the age of the enlightened despot, for the first time attempted to place the heralds under one control and defined their duties, according them an exclusive jurisdiction.

Kings of Arms

As we have seen, the office of 'king of heralds' probably existed as early as the reign of Edward I in 1276. The titles of the present three kings of arms first make their appearance at the end of the fourteenth and the beginning of the fifteenth centuries. Norroy King of Arms, with jurisdiction north of the Trent, is first heard of in 1386 when Richard II appointed a chief herald with that title. In 1420, in the reign of Henry V, we hear for the first time of Clarenceux King of Arms. This chief herald most likely derived his title from close association with the Duke of Clarence (Thomas, Duke of Clarence was the second son of Henry IV) who, as Lord High Constable, had a few years previously been given authority over all the royal heralds. With the decline in influence of the northern earls in this century, and the centralisation of royal power at Westminster, Clarenceux, as the king of arms responsible for heraldic matters south of Trent, came to exercise a power and influence far in excess of his northern colleague. It is true that in the later middle ages the records speak also of other kings of arms, such as March King of Arms, whose title came from the semi-royal Earls of March, but it was Norroy, Clarenceux and Garter who survived.

The first Garter King of Arms was William Bruges, who was appointed in the summer of the year 1415. (See colour illustration, p. 33.) He had been Chester Herald as far back as 1398, and in 1413 had been made Guienne King of Arms (the herald responsible for the ancient duchy of Guienne, or Acquitaine, to which English kings still laid claim). The new title, 'Garter', can be explained by the fact that in that very year 1415 Henry V undertook a revival of the Noble Order of the Garter, at the same time promulgating new statutes for the Knights Companion. One of Bruge's new duties was to record the genealogies of the knights, and to be responsible for the ceremonial ordering of chapters of the order. It seems likely, too, that in October of that same year he was present on the field of Agincourt; in which case he would have had the joyful duty of conducting Mountjoye, the French King of Arms, to his royal master officially to concede the victory.

King of Arms wearing crown

Bruge's responsibilities did not end there, and almost from the first he is found claiming over the other kings of arms and heralds a sovereignty which was often in the years ahead to be disputed, but eventually acknowledged. In 1417, as the result of a petition, the Duke of Clarence, as Constable, decided that whereas in royal processions the heralds were to precede other lords, Garter was to precede the King. Thereafter, the power and influence of holders of this office grew stronger, and one reason may have been that the first two Garters, William Bruges (1415-50) and John Smert (1450-78), had long reigns and were both forceful characters and men of considerable talent. Smert was sent to France as the 'ambassador' of Edward IV to negotiate peace with Louis XI, and as a result of his diplomatic work the two kings were able to meet on the bridge of Picquiny in 1475 to agree to a seven-years truce.

Nevertheless, Garter Kings did not have it all their own way, and succeeding holders of the office were to enter on quarrels, sometimes violent, with the two other kings of arms regarding what the latter called encroachment on their jurisdictions. With Clarenceux the disputing waxed fierce, the southern king of arms claiming that, even if sovereignty over the College of Arms itself be conceded, Garter had no authority to grant arms himself in his province. As considerable sums of money in the way of fees passed each time arms were granted, the acrimonious nature of the dispute can well be imagined. This quarrel came to a climax in the reign of Henry VIII, between Sir Thomas Wriothesley, Garter, and Sir Thomas Benolt, Clarenceux; but peace was patched up on the intervention of the King himself. In 1560 it was agreed that in future grants of arms were to be made in either province by the three kings of arms jointly, and this compromise lasted until after the Restoration. Finally, in 1680, it was settled that in the southern province grants were to be made by Garter and Clarenceux, and in the northern province by Garter and Norroy. This was independent of Garter's general sovereignty over the College of Arms.

Before going on to consider the history of coat armour it is necessary to say something about the organisation of the heralds in a college, and also about the great officers of state to whom they were to become responsible. And since this work is largely concerned with visible symbols of office, there will follow a description and short history of the uniform and insignia worn at various periods by the officers of arms.

The Constable and the Marshal

The Norman and early Angevin royal household was, for administrative purposes, divided into three parts: the courtyard, the hall, and the chamber. In charge of the chamber was the Chamberlain, in charge of the hall was the Steward, and in charge of the courtyard was the Constable. The heralds, once they had developed a separate existence from that of the minstrels, came to belong more naturally to the courtyard, and thus came under the authority of the Constable.

It was not, however, until the reign of Henry V that any direct control seems to have been exercised. As we have seen, it was Thomas, Duke of Clarence, acting officially as Lord High Constable, who settled the matter of precedence among the heralds following the petition of the new Garter King of Arms. The Constable and the Marshal were, in effect, not only great officers of state with important military and political duties at the King's court, but the actual commanders of royal armies. They arranged the order of battle (or at least professionally advised the monarch), and the disposition of the knights and mounted men. They also had charge of tournaments. It followed that in any disputes arising between knights of different regions gathered together for siege or tournament the Constable and Marshal, sitting as a tribunal, acted as a supreme court of appeal. More particularly, this early form of the Court of Chivalry (see below) throughout the fifteenth century determined disputes between contending knights claiming the right to bear similar arms. The fact that Richard III was Lord Constable when he was Duke of Gloucester may well have stimulated that personal interest which, when he became King, resulted in the grant of the heralds' first charter.

The last High Constable of England was Edward Stafford, Duke of Buckingham, who was unfortunate enough to end his career and his life by way of the block in 1521. It was the Duke's misfortune that he was not only the first nobleman of the land, but was also of royal Plantagenet blood at a time when there was no male heir to the Tudor throne. A stupid quarrel with 'the butcher's son' and a trumped-up charge of treason effectively removed this threat to the dynasty, and it seems that Henry VIII thereafter deliberately refrained from conferring so mighty an office on another subject. The result was that the Constable's powers and jurisdiction over heraldic matters passed permanently to his deputy, the Marshal. Until 1533 this office was held by Charles Brandon, Duke of Suffolk, the King's old jousting companion who had married his sister, the Princess Mary. Suffolk was succeeded by Thomas, third Duke of Norfolk, the Lord Treasurer. Arrested and condemned to death for suspected treason (his own son, the poet Earl of Surrey, did suffer the supreme penalty), the Duke escaped execution through the lucky chance of the King himself dying before he could sign the death warrant. Although Norfolk spent most of the next reign in the Tower, he resumed his Marshal's duties for a short time on the accession of Queen Mary Tudor.

On his death in 1554 he was succeeded by his grandson, the fourth duke. This cultured nobleman was less lucky than his grandfather, suffering execution at the hands of Elizabeth's government for his part in the Catholic Northern Rising in 1572; but not before he had been responsible for two very important landmarks in the history of the heralds: the Charter of 1555, and the Orders of 1568. These events will be discussed in the next section.

After the Duke's death, the office of Earl Marshal was for a time put into commission, and then bestowed on various noblemen for the next hundred years. In 1672, Charles II appointed Henry Howard, Earl of Norwich, Earl Marshal with hereditary right of succession. The following year Henry Howard succeeded his brother as Duke of Norfolk, the greater title of the Howard family, lost by the attainder of the Elizabethan duke, having been restored by Charles II in 1662. This new duke was to exercise a not inconsiderable influence over the fortunes of the heralds' college. At the beginning of the eighteenth century the Duke of Norfolk of the time returned to the Catholic faith of his ancestors, and one very important result was that, because of the Test Act, he and his successors were obliged to execute their office through a series of deputies until repeal of the Act in 1827. Nevertheless, it was usually contrived that the deputies should be Protestant nominees—often members of the Howard family—who were prepared to defer to the dukes and allow them to exercise considerable influence behind the scenes. The Dukes of Norfolk have continued to hold this office, often with distinction, and the present Earl Marshal has held it for more than fifty years (though as a minor for the first years), and has been responsible for two coronations, the state funerals of George V, George VI and Sir Winston Churchill and, latest of all, the investiture of the present Prince of Wales at Caernarvon Castle in 1969.

The College of Arms: 1 Beginnings

The first charter of incorporation for the heralds was granted by Richard III in March 1483/84. The charter, which was addressed to 'John Writhe, Garter, Thomas Holme, Clarenceux, John Blore, Norroy, Richard Champney, Gloucester King of Arms of Wales, and all other heralds and pursuivants of arms' constituted these officers of arms and their successors in office a 'body corporate with perpetual succession and a common seal'. It also granted the heralds for the first time a home. They were given a house called Coldharbour, in the City of London, where they might meet and keep their records and books. The importance with which the heralds at this time were regarded can be gauged from the fact that Coldharbour was one of the greatest houses in the City. Built in the fourteenth century by Sir John Pultney, four times mayor of London, and builder also of Penshurst Hall, the house had passed into the hands of a succession of owners whose names read like a chronicle of English history—William de Montagu, Earl of Salisbury; Humphrey de Bohun, Earl of Hereford; Henry IV; Henry V as Prince of Wales; and John Holland, Duke of Exeter. Three years before King Richard granted the heralds Coldharbour, Margaret, Duchess of Burgundy, sister of Richard, and his brother, Edward IV, had lodged there during a 'state' visit to England. At Coldharbour now were stored the earliest records of the college, the medieval books and rolls of arms. A further point of interest is the opinion of Sir Anthony Wagner, the present Garter King of Arms, that the arms of the college were granted by Richard III at the same time that he gave the charter, and were used for the common seal: 'Argent, a cross gules, in each quarter a dove azure with one wing open and the other close beaked and legged gules'.

Sadly, the heralds were to occupy their splendid new home for only eighteen months. One of the results of the slaying of the last Plantagenet king at Bosworth was that the new Tudor monarch, Henry VII, expelled them in order to present Coldharbour to his mother, the Lady Margaret Beaufort. The heralds themselves suffered varying fortunes, no doubt reflecting their degrees of loyalty to their dead patron, but Garter Writhe survived, and although on his death in 1504 Henry VII wished to confer the title of Clarenceux on Roger Machado, who had been his 'Richmond King of Arms' in the days of his exile, Machado, now an old man, declined the honour; whereupon the King was easily persuaded to appoint Writhe's son, Thomas. It was this Thomas who changed the family name to Wriothesley[1], a name famous in history not only for his own long reign as Garter King of Arms, but also for the line founded by his nephew, William, who rose to be Henry VIII's Lord Chancellor, first Earl of Southampton, and the ancestor of Shakespeare's patron. During the next fifty years the heralds had no home of their own, and carried out their duties from the royal palaces, following the court as it moved about. Indeed, Henry VII made an order as early as 1487 requiring a king of arms, a herald and a pursuivant to attend court in rotation, serving a month and a half at a time. The immediate fate of the precious rolls and records is obscure, though Sir Anthony Wagner brings to light evidence to suggest that they remained in the possession of Garter Writhe, and afterwards of his son, Garter Wriothesley. If chapter meetings of the heralds were held at Garter's private residence, this seems their likely fate.

The College of Arms: 2 New Foundation

On 18 July 1555 Thomas, fourth Duke of Norfolk, who had succeeded Henry VIII's Lord Treasurer as Earl Marshal, secured from Queen Mary Tudor and her consort King Philip a charter which, in effect, gave the heralds a new foundation and the official position they hold to this day. The charter enacted the following:

(*a*) The College was to consist of the existing body of heralds, namely, Garter, Clarenceux and Norroy Kings of Arms; Windsor, Chester, Richmond, Somerset, York and Lancaster Heralds; Rouge Croix, Blue Mantle, Rouge Dragon and Portcullis Pursuivants. These with 'all other heralds and pursuivants and their successors' to constitute 'a corporation with perpetual succession'.

(*b*) As a new home they were granted 'Derby Place in the parishes of St Benet and St Peter in the way leading from the south door of St Paul's Cathedral to Paul's Wharf, that they might keep safe their records and rolls and all other things touching their faculty'.

A touch of poetic justice may be seen in the coincidence that Derby Place had been built by the second husband of Lady Margaret Beaufort who, in 1485, had acquired the heralds' original home. This husband was Thomas Stanley, who had been rewarded for his treachery at Bosworth by the grant of the earldom of Derby.

On 18 July 1568 the same Duke of Norfolk, as Earl Marshal, promulgated a series of orders which were to have a profound influence on the future history of the College of Arms. Three important principles were now established:

(i)   The ultimate authority of the Earl Marshal over the heralds was, in effect, to be absolute. No chapters were to be held except in his presence, and all orders agreed on by the heralds were to be confirmed by him.

(ii) All 'records, rolls, books and pedigrees' were to be kept at Derby Place, nor could any be removed without the consent of Garter and at least one other king of arms. The exception allowed was that Clarenceux and Norroy might take with them on official Visitations such books as might be relevant, provided they were returned to the college at the end of the Visitation.

(*iii*) To ensure the safe custody of the records, the orders stipulated that no one should be allowed to enter the college 'without one officer of arms be there present with him'. To make this possible it was further laid down that, by monthly rotation, two officers were to make daily attendance. Except that 'monthly' was altered to 'weekly' in 1912, this remains the rule today.

Less than three years later this cultured and enlightened Earl Marshal suffered, as we have seen, the fate of so many of his family in that dangerous century, and for a time it seemed that, lacking a strong hand at the helm, the college unity might disintegrate into quarrelling groups. To some extent this was prevented by the long reigns and personalities of the Elizabethan Garters, Sir Gilbert Dethick (1550-84) and his son, Sir William Dethick (1586-1606), which did much to preserve continuity in the college. Another factor which undoubtedly helped to maintain its prestige was that in Robert Glover, Somerset Herald, the college had at that time a scholar of great eminence. Sir Anthony Wagner has written of this herald that his manuscript collections attest 'a critical and scholarly approach without parallel among his contemporaries'. Lastly, from 1597 to 1623, spanning the transition from Tudor to Stuart times, the important office of Clarenceux King of Arms was in the hands of one of the greatest figures of the age, the antiquarian William Camden.

The college survived the troubled times of Charles I and the Civil War, though during the period of the Commonwealth the heralds were divided in their allegiance. Some fled into exile to join the young King Charles II, while others remained to make their peace with the Parliament. Sir Edward Walker, who had been appointed Garter by Charles I in 1644 when the King was hardly in a position to exercise much influence on heraldic or any other affairs, loyally went into exile. When, following the execution of the King, the Commonwealth was set up, it might have been expected that the republicans would have had no use for the trappings of heraldry; but, strange to relate, the opposite proved to be the case. Commissioners were appointed to select suitable persons to constitute their own Court of Chivalry, and in October 1649 'Edward Bishe Esquire, a Member of the House' was appointed Garter. One of his first duties seems to have been to arrange the funeral in Westminster Abbey of the third Earl of Essex, the former Lord General of the Parliamentary Army.

At the Restoration, Sir Edward Walker, back from exile, was confirmed in office as Garter, while Bishe, who seems to have adopted the more aristocratic spelling of his name as 'Bysshe', was compensated for his loss by being given a knighthood and the office of Clarenceux, in which office he continued until his death in 1679. But his work, at any rate in respect of Visitations, appears to have been far from satisfactory. On two occasions he was called to account, and in 1675 was prohibited by the Deputy Earl Marshal from any visiting at all. To turn to the brighter side, the college in this period numbered among its officers a herald of national repute, Elias Ashmole, who is best known for his foundation of the museum that bears his name at Oxford University, and for his great history of the Order of the Garter. Ashmole was Windsor Herald from 1660 until he resigned in 1675. The eighteenth century produced two outstanding Garter Kings of Arms whose work and influence, despite a long-standing quarrel, raised the college to new heights of prestige. (See below: Court of Chivalry and Order of the Bath). A curious detail to be noted is that at the beginning of this century the office of Clarenceux King of Arms was held by Sir John Vanburgh for some years. His work as a herald does not appear to have been particularly successful, and no doubt he was content to allow his reputation to rest on his genius as an architect and playwright.

But history is not concerned only with the members of the College of Arms. In September 1666 disaster struck, and among the buildings of London destroyed by the Great Fire was Derby Place. Fortunately, nearly all the records, rolls and books were saved and conveyed to Whitehall, where they were given a temporary home. It is interesting to speculate whether the young Pepys, inspecting the progress of the flames through the City, may not have witnessed the officers of arms laden with their precious records coming out of Derby Place before he returned to Seething Lane to supervise the removal of the equally important Navy records. The rebuilding of Derby Place on the same site was to occupy many years. The library was completed in 1675 and the books and records moved in, but largely through lack of funds further building was held up. By 1683 the north and west sides of the new building, comprising thirty-seven rooms, were complete. But further building was to go on until 1748. Early in Queen Victoria's reign a new record room was added, but the present College of Arms is substantially the building erected in the late seventeenth century. Now the premises are being extended to include a museum.

The Court of Chivalry

Known officially in the middle ages as 'Curia Militaris', this court is generally believed to have come into existence in 1347/48, when the Curia Regis delegated to the Constable and Marshal power to settle disputes and hear cases 'touching deeds of arms and of war out of the realm, and also of things that touch (arms or) war within the realm, which cannot be discussed by the common law . . .' Over a hundred years before the heralds had a corporate existence, such disputes were settled by these two great officers of state sitting as a court and deriving their authority from the royal prerogative. No doubt the royal heralds customarily attended sessions of this 'court' when their evidence and professional advice must have been required. But the authority was not theirs but the Constable's, and after he disappeared from the scene, the Earl Marshal's. Nevertheless, in the sixteenth and early seventeenth centuries that authority was sometimes disputed. Particularly did this happen in King James's reign, when it was fashionable to attack the royal prerogative generally, at least as it was interpreted by King James himself.

The Court of Chivalry, as we may now call it, being a prerogative court as much as Star Chamber or High Commission, came in for its share of attack, largely over the question of jurisdiction. It must be remembered that, originally, the court had been set up to deal with cases outside the jurisdiction of the common law of England, and it was sometimes difficult to know where to draw the line. The Puritans, whose influence was becoming very powerful at this time, were staunch upholders of the common law against the royal prerogative and no doubt this defiance of royal authority played its part in a dispute which arose in 1621. In that year Thomas, Earl of Arundel, who would have been Duke of Norfolk but for the attainder of Elizabeth's Parliament, was made Earl Marshal for life. For some years previously the leader of the opposition to the Marshal's authority in the court had been Ralph Brooke, York Herald since 1592. Brooke had been joined by Robert Treswell, who had been appointed Somerset Herald in 1594, and these two stirred up trouble by litigation and other means, seeking to prove that the Marshal had no legal power to take to himself that authority which had formerly belonged to the High Constable (it will be remembered there had been no Constable since the execution of the Duke of Buckingham in 1521). The year after Arundel became Marshal, James I, who saw in these attacks a reflection on his own honour, referred the whole matter to the Privy Council. In July 1622 the council reported unanimously that, in the vacancy in the office of Lord High Constable, the Earl Marshal had power to judge all causes belonging to the jurisdiction of the Court of Constable and Marshal. The King, therefore, on 1 August in the same year, made a formal declaration of the Marshal's authority and directed him to 'restore and settle his court's procedure'. The result was that between 1622 and the opening of the Civil War twenty years later the Court of Chivalry enjoyed its greatest period of prosperity and power.

At the Restoration, although the royal heralds came into their own again, the Court of Chivalry suffered an eclipse. This was partly because, until 1672, the office of Earl Marshal was in commission, and partly because Sir Edward Walker, Garter King of Arms, was maintaining the traditional quarrel with the other kings of arms; first with Sir Edward Bysshe whom we have already met, and later with Sir William Dugdale, Norroy, who was to succeed Walker after his death. The appointment of the future Duke of Norfolk, Henry Howard, as Earl Marshal in 1672 with right of hereditary succession, and his revival of the Orders of 1568, went far to restoring the authority of the court. When in 1688, with the expulsion of the Stuart kings, Visitations came to an end it might have been thought that the chief reason for the court's existence had ceased. In fact, it was active throughout the reign of William III, giving judgements in many prosecutions against persons charged with displaying arms on funeral hatchments and in other public places without authority. A point that should be mentioned is that not only were those who made use of unauthorised arms liable to prosecution, but also the heraldic painters. Heraldic painting was a specialised art, and those men skilled in it had long won for themselves a privileged position because of their long experience and knowledge. One consequence was that armigerous-minded persons who, for one reason or another, did not formally apply for grants of arms often consulted the painters over the actual design. Further, the painters were sometimes consulted on details of funeral ceremony which, in those days, reflected in no small degree the social position of the family. The concern of the heralds at this encroachment on their authority can easily be appreciated, *and* their satisfaction at possessing a court to deal with it.

The disqualification of Thomas, Duke of Norfolk, who succeeded his uncle Henry in 1701, first as a minor then from 1704 as a Catholic convert, meant that the duties of Earl Marshal had to be performed by a deputy. In effect, there were to be five different deputies during the course of the next thirty years, with the consequence that the court lost a great deal of its prestige. But in 1732 the Duke chose for his deputy his own kinsman, Lord Howard of Effingham, who was created an earl in his own right to qualify him for that office. The Earl Marshalship being in one family again, as it were, the old duke determined through his deputy to revive the ancient glories of the court and restore generally the power and influence of the heralds. Unfortunately, as so often happened, during the critical period the two greatest figures of the College of Arms in the eighteenth century were at loggerheads— Sir John Anstis, Garter 1715-44, and Sir Stephen Martin Leake, Norroy, and Garter from 1754 to 1773. One cause of their quarrel arose over the precedence Anstis wished to give to his revival of the ancient Order of the Bath (see Chapter 5). Nevertheless, the Court of Chivalry did assemble again in the courtroom of the college in the year 1732 on 30 March, 25 April, 8 May, 23 May, and 3 June. The revival had been preceded on 3 March by a procession to the Painted Chamber of the old House of Lords, where it was resolved that the Court of Chivalry should assemble in due course at the College of Arms to determine certain causes. The magnificence of the procession on this occasion reflected its importance. First went the Crier and Usher, then the Proctors, followed by the Doctors of Civil Law in black gowns. Next came the Earl Marshal's Proctor, the Register and the King's Advocate. They were followed by the heralds in order of seniority, Garter and Norroy (Anstis and Leake) bringing up the rear, but preceding the Deputy Earl Marshal with his stave of office. Following this first part of the procession came sixteen peers of the realm, the Lord President of the Council, and the Lord Great Chamberlain, all in their Parliament robes. Last of all came the Earl Marshal's Surrogate and Assessor in the scarlet robes of a doctor. This last person no doubt owed his position of honour in the procession to the fact that he was to preside over the court at all its sittings except that on 8 May when the Deputy Earl Marshal was present. (See the famous painting of this scene by Gilroy.)

Three cases were brought before the court, but both Anstis and Leake, in accord for once, came to the conclusion that in the absence of Visitations it was impossible for the Surrogate to arrive at a proper conclusion, and so they advised. A movement was set on foot to revive Visitations which, it will be remembered, had ceased in 1688, but it came to nothing. In the meantime two of the persons prosecuted moved through their counsel a prohibition against the Court of

Page 33   The first Garter King of Arms, William Bruges, appointed in 1415

Page 34   The King's Champion escorted by the Lord High Steward and the Lord High Constable in their Coronation robes

Chivalry in the King's Bench. This trial of prohibition was not settled until 1734. The Duke of Norfolk had died in December 1732, and his successor re-appointed Lord Effingham as deputy and instructed him to continue the sittings of the court. Nothing much was accomplished owing to cross petitions to the Court of Chancery, and the Court of Chivalry sat for the last time for over two centuries on 4 March 1737.

In 1954 Manchester City Corporation petitioned the present Earl Marshal to re-convene the Court of Chivalry to hear a complaint that a local cinema was, without authority, displaying the city arms. After consideration and advice he agreed and the court assembled on 21 December 1954, not in the Earl Marshal's hall at the College of Arms, but in the court of the Lord Chief Justice at the Royal Courts of Justice in the Strand. This place of assembly was chosen, says Sir Anthony Wagner who had much to do with the arrangements, because of the number of persons wishing to attend the proceedings. On the invitation of the Earl Marshal, the Lord Chief Justice (Lord Goddard) presided as Surrogate. Sir Anthony has described the scene: 'The Earl Marshal in levée dress (scarlet tunic with dark blue trousers and gold stripe) sat on the bench with the Surrogate, who wore the scarlet robes and bonnet of an Oxford Doctor of Civil Law. Heralds and Pursuivants were present in uniform (not tabards?), and I as joint Register of the Court (with Mr W. M. Phillips, notary public) sat below the bench and recited the Earl Marshal's style and extracts from the letters patent of 19 October 1672.'

The hearing occupied two days. In his judgement on behalf of the Earl Marshal, the Surrogate made two suggestions:

(*i*) That to prevent in future frivolous actions, leave should first be obtained before any proceedings were instituted.

(*ii*) That he (Lord Goddard) was of the opinion now that the Court of Chivalry had been revived, that it should 'be put on a statutory basis, defining its jurisdiction and the sanctions it can impose.'

Seventeen years have passed since the Court of Chivalry last assembled, and, so far as is known, there has been no move to ask Parliament to implement the late Lord Goddard's advice. In Scotland, the Lord Lyon King of Arms's judgements in respect of those matters falling within his jurisdiction have the force of statute law, but this has never been the case in England. Perhaps there is no need. In all its long history the College of Arms has managed to survive every crisis in its affairs, and to emerge with its prestige and influence as great as ever they were.

2 : Origins and History of Coat Armour

The charter of Richard III, to which reference has already been made, contained three important clauses:

(*i*)   The heralds were to take note of all arms existing at the time; that is, to make a complete record which was to be kept at the new College of Arms.

(*ii*)   The heralds were to allow no new arms without authority; that is, to see that no one displayed arms to which they could not prove they were entitled.

(*iii*)   The heralds were enjoined to grant arms only to those whose ancestry proved them to be gentlemen, or who by marriage or possession of sufficient wealth could be said to have entered the class of landed gentry.

What were these 'arms' and how did they originate? Sir Anthony Wagner says: 'Armorial bearings were first adopted by the knights, for whom between the twelfth century and the fourteenth they fulfilled a practical military purpose'. But the practice may have begun even earlier. The shield, whatever its shape, was the obvious surface background for painted patterns and designs in colour; and taking no account of what Greek, Roman and Eastern warriors may have attempted in earlier ages, there is no doubt that those great soldiers, the Normans, painted designs on their kite-shaped shields in the eleventh century. The Bayeux Tapestry clearly shows geometric patterns and beasts on the shields of the Norman knights. We may take it, however, that it was not until the twelfth century that any definite system was followed. By the time of Richard Coeur de Lion there had arisen a special reason for keeping watch on shield designs. Until this reign, battles and sieges had been fought by knights wearing chain mail but with the face left uncovered by the rounded steel helmet of the day. Now it was becoming fashionable to protect the face by wearing a helmet with a visor that was pulled down when fighting actually started. With the face now concealed and the body armour worn by both sides differing hardly at all, in the confusion of battle it became impossible to distinguish between friend and foe. If, therefore, some system could be devised for keeping records, with the double object of providing identification and preventing duplication, a great deal of confusion and of actual danger might be avoided. And so was born the roll of arms.

The Roll of Arms

These were long rolls of parchment on which were reproduced miniature copies in colour of knightly shields attested by brief statements beneath each. It is impossible at this distance of time to say who first thought of the idea; it seems to have been adopted in France, England and other countries of western Europe more or less simultaneously. This is not so remarkable a coincidence as might be supposed. In the twelfth century the national state was in its infancy. Allegiance was to the feudal lord rather than to the State, which would in any event be hard to define. Moreover, many lords held lands in more than one country. There was, too, a common language of chivalry, French. A few copies of early rolls still existing are of great value to scholars studying medieval history. In England two such rolls spring to mind: Glover's Roll (named after the Elizabethan herald) which contains some 250 shields and was compiled about the year 1255 in the reign of Henry III; and the Great Roll which was compiled about the year 1308 in the reign of Edward II and contains over eleven hundred shields. It is reasonable to suppose that the number of rolls multiplied thereafter as occasion demanded. And now we have to consider how the heralds came to be associated with this keeping of records and the control of future grants of arms.

Grants of Arms

In the beginning, the right to bear arms seems to have been restricted to tenants-in-chief of the King, that is to the great feudal earls and barons. To this class must be added the diocesan bishops and abbots of the greater monasteries. In those days this class of churchman ranked as barons and held land on the same feudal terms. Very soon these great lords began to grant arms to their own followers, known as 'mesne tenants', who held land on condition of military service to their lords or sometimes to the King direct. This was the 'knight' class, and the Crusades, the Hundred Years War and, from the middle of the thirteenth century, the increasing popularity of the tournament, resulted in a large increase in the number of knights entitled to bear arms. In England, the glorification of chivalry by Edward III after Crecy, and his creation of the Knights of the Garter at Windsor to extol the valour and virtues of King Arthur and his Knights of the Round Table as contemporary thought pictured them, did much to enhance the status of this class of subject. It became, therefore, a matter of considerable importance to find a suitable body of officials to check the *bona fides* of existing arms and to control the grant of new ones. It was fortunate that in the heralds there already existed such a body well suited for this work. By the year 1400 the heralds had become the acknowledged experts on armorial bearings, though they did not yet have the exclusive right to grant new arms.

Not the least of the difficulties confronting them in the task of bringing the records to some sort of order was the practice of great lords of conferring on favoured subordinates the right to bear their their own arms or some portion of them. By this time, too, arms were being adopted, often illegally, by towns, guild companies and wealthy merchants. Naturally, all this caused a great deal of confusion and it is not surprising that, long before the end of the century, the heralds had won for themselves an almost exclusive right both to devise arms and to assign them. In this England departed from the continental practice. In France, for example, it was the King who usually made the grant which was then 'registered' by the French kings of arms. The long-term result of this was that the French heralds gradually lost most of their influence until Henry IV virtually removed control of the grant of arms from them altogether. In England, on the other hand, we find very few examples of direct royal grants of arms. In 1394 Richard II granted to Thomas Mowbray, then Earl of Nottingham, the royal crest of 'a leopard or differenced with a crown argent round the neck'. When, a few years later, Mowbray was created Duke of Norfolk, and was by the laws of chivalry entitled to new arms, the King granted him the right to impale the arms of St Edward (the Confessor) with his own Mowbray arms. Succeeding Kings of England made very few direct grants, the most notable being by Henry VI to his own foundations, eg, Eton College.

That it was thought necessary to embody the direction given in the third clause quoted above of King Richard's charter—'to grant arms only to those whose ancestry proved them to be gentlemen, or who by marriage or possession of sufficient wealth could be said to have entered the class of landed gentry'—throws a sharp, clear light on the armorial situation towards the end of the fifteenth century. More settled times, and above all the rapid growth in wealth and influence of a new middle class, had brought about a remarkable increase in the numbers of those seeking in this way public recognition of their improved social status. As we should put it today, everyone was trying to climb on the bandwagon of respectability, and in the fifteenth/sixteenth centuries the outward sign was the possession of a coat of arms,

not for display in battle but in carved stone over the gatehouse of the
newly acquired estate, painted on the overmantel in the great hall, and
sculpted over the family memorial in the parish church. Few of these
people could prove descent from noble or even gentle ancestry. In the
words of the charter, they sought to enter the class of landed gentry
through the acquisition of land. The Reformation and the dissolution
of the English monasteries a few years later gave them their greatest
opportunity, and it is common knowledge that most of the great Whig
families politically and socially important in English history of the
seventeenth and eighteenth centuries originated in humble ancestors
who had made themselves wealthy and socially acceptable by the purchase
in the sixteenth century of confiscated monastic land. Such a family was
the Cecils. One thinks also of families like the Cavendishes, the
Seymours, the Wriothesleys,[2] the Herberts and the Greshams, all of
whom rose to positions of eminence around this time. It followed that
the heralds were kept very busy with this side of their work, and, as
might be expected, they were to find that many persons were displaying
arms to which they had no right. In a very class-conscious society such
a situation could not be tolerated, and so from the time of the reign of
Henry VIII there began a series of Visitations that were to continue
until 1688.

The Visitations

To write a detailed account of sixteenth- and seventeenth-century
Visitations is outside the scope of this book. The whole history is set
forth most authoritatively by Sir Anthony Wagner in *Heralds of
England*. We may, however, note a few of the highlights.

In the early years, the manner of carrying out these Visitations was
the cause of stormy dispute between Garter and the two other kings
of arms. In 1539, a chapter of heralds held at Westminster decided that
Garter King of Arms must make no visitations himself, but he was
confirmed in his right to 'correct' the arms and crests of Knights of the
Garter. In the Duke of Norfolk's orders of 1568 it was laid down that
in future every patent of arms was to be signed by all three kings of
arms jointly. The order seems to have lapsed during the troubled
years of Charles I and the Commonwealth which followed, but in 1673
the new Earl Marshal (Henry Howard, Duke of Norfolk) restored it,
and made it mandatory that all grants of arms were to be made 'only
by the three kings of arms jointly', and, further, that they were to be
on the Earl Marshal's warrant under 'his hand and seal'. This order

was modified later, as we have seen, in 1680, when it was then decided that grants were to be made by Garter and Clarenceux in the southern province, and by Garter and Norroy in the northern province.

Today, when Visitations no longer take place, a right to arms can only be established by the applicant registering in the official records of the College of Arms a pedigree showing direct male descent from an ancestor already appearing in the college records as being entitled to arms, or, alternatively, by making a personal application for a grant of new arms. In this latter case he will, presumably, have to satisfy the kings of arms that he is a person of sufficient substance, though one imagines that the original requirement of having 'entered the class of landed gentry' is treated more liberally than it would have been in earlier centuries. It will be remembered that from early times individuals were not the only applicants for grants of arms. The universities, corporations of new charter towns, and merchant guilds were numbered among those who officially acquired arms. In the sixteenth century they were also granted to a few of the merchant trading companies, to professional bodies such as the barber-surgeons' company, and to university colleges, though sometimes permission was granted for such foundations to display the arms of their founders. In our own age there has been a revival of such corporate applications, as is shown by the arms borne by such bodies as the British Broadcasting Corporation, the National Coal Board, and others.

In the time of Visitations the actual work was carried out by the two provincial kings attended by other heralds and pursuivants. In the sixteenth century the custom seems to have been for the sheriff, on the Earl Marshal's warrant, to summon the gentry of each hundred of the county to appear before the king of arms of the province and his colleagues in the house of one of their number. All who, on report, were shown to have made use of arms were obliged to submit evidence to prove they were entitled to bear them. Newcomers who had as yet received no grant submitted pedigrees, or evidence of wealth and fitness.

Finally, persons who had been reported to be bearing arms without authority were brought before the heralds, and, if found guilty, were fined, or even imprisoned if the offence were judged serious enough. Clarenceux and Norroy on these progresses carried with them, as we have noted, the appropriate books and rolls, which they returned to the college at the end of the Visitation.

3 : Ceremonial Dress and Insignia

Evolution of the Tabard

The magnificent scarlet, blue and gold tabards quartered with the royal arms which the heralds wear on state occasions are today, thanks to television and newspaper photographs, familiar to millions of the Queen's subjects. We have now to discover how they evolved—tabards, gold collars, rods and (for coronations only) the crowns of the kings of arms.

In the middle ages there were no uniforms in the modern sense, just as there were no professional armies or navies. But by the thirteenth century it had become customary for servants to wear coats embroidered or painted with their master's arms, and this custom was followed by the heralds. At this date knights not in armour wore two tunics: an inner garment reaching to the ankles, with long tight-fitting sleeves, and an outer tunic, called the 'surcoat', which was almost as long, but without sleeves. The surcoat had been brought back from the East by the Crusaders who copied the Saracens in wearing it over their chain mail as a protection against the heat of the sun's rays. The Crusading knights took to blazoning their arms on the front of this garment, and the early heralds wearing their master's coat did likewise.

The next stage in the evolution of the heralds' costume was the 'jupon', a much shorter and more close-fitting form of garment. The shortness of the tunic—it was with time to become as short as a modern mini-skirt—resulted in a new form of long hose being worn with it, sewn together at the fork, and a codpiece. This fashion reached its apogee in the reign of Richard II, under whose patronage fashions in clothes became fantastic by earlier standards. But almost immediately it seemed that men began to regret showing so much of themselves because the jupon, or doublet, began to grow longer.

The 'tabard' made its appearance in the fifteenth century, and took the form of an outer garment with very full short sleeves. Still following the medieval custom of servants wearing their master's coats, the heralds now took to wearing this garment. But this time, when lay fashion again changed, they continued wearing the tabard, which of course carried on it the arms of their masters. Much in the same way did judges continue to wear wigs after everyone else had discarded them in the seventeen-nineties.

Perhaps the disappearance of the heralds of the noble households around this time had something to do with this decision. The royal

Pursuivant with tabard worn athwart

heralds, newly incorporated as an official body, might have wished to
draw attention to their unique status by the retention of a garment
eminently suited to their purpose long after lay persons had abandoned
its use. It is thought that Henry VII was the last English monarch to
wear a tabard (was he wearing one at Bosworth?), and another reason
may have been that the king's heralds saw in the perpetuation of the

tabard with its blazoning of the royal arms a constant reminder of the diplomatic status they had achieved. We may note that at this time the royal arms were those of England (gules three leopards or passant guardant) quartered with those of France (azure three fleur-de-lys or). A curious custom which lasted until almost the end of the sixteenth century was for the pursuivants to wear their tabards athwart, that is with the long pieces at the sides with short full sleeve pieces fore and aft. Many contemporary illustrations show this clearly, and it is evident that this was the custom all over western Europe.

The Material of Tabards

The medieval tabard, following contemporary lay fashion, was made of wool and lined with fur, or at least fur-edged. By the middle years of Henry VIII's reign the heralds of noble houses were no more, and in 1544 certain instructions were issued with regard to materials to be used henceforth for the tabards of royal heralds:

Kings of Arms	satin
Heralds	damask
Pursuivants	sarsenet (fine soft silk)

Two further changes were to be made. In Elizabeth I's reign it was ordered that kings of arms must wear velvet tabards, and in James I's reign that heralds must wear satin.

Under-Garments of Heralds

In the earliest age of heralds, their under-garment was doubtless the long tunic with close-fitting sleeves of contemporary lay fashion. Over this, as we have seen, was worn the surcoat, the 'livery' which in feudal Europe lords gave to their servants as an essential part of their maintenance. On the principle that servants by the smartness of their turnout reflect the social status of their masters, it was natural for those masters to see to it that the livery did not conceal threadbare or shabby under-garments. There is plenty of evidence in the form of surviving accounts to prove a considerable expenditure on cloth for these servants and retainers. Illustrations from the thirteenth to the fifteenth century suggest that heralds followed contemporary fashion in under-garments, and towards the end of this period were wearing under their tabards short, close-fitting tunics and long hose. (See illustration of Garter Smert reproduced in Wagner's *Heralds of England*). As has been noted, when lay fashion changed again the heralds continued to wear the tabard which has ever since remained their livery of office; but with

Herald in hood, tabard and undergarment

the coming of the Tudors they appear to have adopted as an under-
garment the long full robe open down the front and reaching to the
feet which, in lay circles, was now worn only by elderly persons and
certain officials. They continued to wear this form of under-garment
throughout the sixteenth century, and at least on special occasions
during the seventeenth. An illustration of the funeral of the first Duke of
Albermarle (more familiar as General George Monk) shows the heralds

in procession wearing the long robe under their tabards. This illustration also shows in the front opening of the robe that they wore full breeches to the knee and stockings, the lay fashion of the day.

In the next century the heralds adopted contemporary lay costume consisting of breeches to the knee, stockings and buckled shoes, embroidered waistcoat and skirted coat. No doubt the material and lacing would be of the best, and it seems that an attempt was made to ensure that all heralds wore the same colour and embroidery. This was perhaps the beginning of an attempt to produce the first uniform, and it was this same eighteenth century that saw the genesis of modern military and naval uniforms.

It was not until the nineteenth century that any recognisable uniform in the modern sense made its appearance at the College of Arms. George IV, as is well known, had decided views on dress; but for great state occasions, including his own coronation, he seems to have tried to put the clock back by dressing as many officials as possible in his own version of what the Tudor courts wore. In 1831, however, a royal warrant of William IV approved a dark blue uniform with military trousers to match for the heralds. In 1849 Queen Victoria gave her approval to the wearing of a levée dress consisting of the scarlet tunic still worn on high state occasions. Finally, by royal warrants of 1902 and 1906, Edward VII laid it down that black breeches and stockings with silver buckled shoes (and scarlet tunic) should be worn under the tabard. At the coronations of George VI and Elizabeth II white satin breeches with white silk stockings and gold-buckled court shoes were worn; but for other ceremonial occasions the heralds still adhere to the regulations of Edward VII.

Head Dress

From the earliest times heraldic head dress seems to have faithfully followed lay fashion. In the fourteenth century this was the hood, usually with liripipe. Contemporary illustration shows, however, that heralds then very often did not actually wear the hood over the head, but hanging down the back. This hood had a roll-top base forming a short cape round the shoulders and neck.

In the early fifteenth century the heralds adopted the Burgundian tall cap. Illustrations of heralds wearing this form of headgear show how well suited to the dignity of the office this cap was, but unfortunately, it was eventually abandoned in favour of the black velvet cap of Edward IV's time.

Fifteenth-century herald wearing Burgundian cap

This cap, which developed into the Tudor square cap or 'quadratus' with or without ear flaps, became by Elizabethan times the common head dress of officials. The heralds are, however, in this age often shown bare-headed, and no doubt they sometimes carried their caps in their hands. A curious fact to be noted is that the medieval hood had not disappeared altogether, for illustrations of the funerals of Sir Philip

Sidney (1586), and of the Duke of Albemarle already referred to, which took place almost a hundred years later, both show the heralds wearing medieval hoods over their heads. It would appear that the wearing of these hoods was confined to state funerals and therefore must have been a form of official mourning.

During the eighteenth century the heralds again followed the contemporary lay fashion by adopting the tricorn, which they wore over the wigs to which, like everyone else, they had taken in the previous century. Unlike the royal judges and counsel, the heralds discarded the wig, as did most lay persons, when William Pitt introduced his powder tax in 1793. No doubt this was meant as a patriotic gesture—as royal servants they might have retained their wigs. The tricorn, of course, also disappeared from use, and the heralds seem generally to have adopted the half-moon or sickle hat made fashionable by the Directory, though they may often have gone bare-headed, as many illustrations up to the time of George IV seem to show.

The black velvet cap in a rather different shape was restored by Edward VII, who had definite views of his own on sartorial matters, and was worn up to and including the Proclamation ceremonies of Edward VIII and George VI in 1936. Today the English heralds usually wear a type of cocked hat, placed fore and aft and set with feathers from peak to peak. For kings of arms the feathers are white, for heralds and pursuivants black.

Crowns and Insignia

It has been noted that the title 'king' of heralds appeared as early as the year 1276, and some early heraldic seals also show this symbol. By the fourteenth and fifteenth centuries kings of arms were actually being crowned at their inauguration, a ceremony which may have had its origins in the medieval custom of 'crowning' popularly elected 'kings' to preside over the many seasonal feastings in which our medieval forebears used to delight. Of such was the Bean King at Twelfth Night, the May King to welcome Spring, and the Lord of Misrule at Christmas. From at least the middle of the fourteenth century there was another ceremony for heralds, that of baptism, when they had officially bestowed on them their names of office taken from the names, lordships or armorial devices of their masters (eg, Exeter Herald, Blanche Sanglier Pursuivant, etc.) This baptism involved pouring over them a little water from a silver or silver-gilt cup, and then solemnly investing them with the robe or tabard blazoned with the lord's arms. By the fifteenth century it had become customary to use an open silver cup for the baptism of pursuivants, for heralds an open silver-gilt cup, and for kings of arms a silver-gilt cup with embossed lid.

The earliest pictorial representation of a king of arms wearing his crown depicts William Bruge, the first Garter. This 'portrait' is a full-page illumination in the Stowe MS now in the British Museum and shows the kneeling herald praying to St George. The crown the artist has given him is very elaborate. It has two engrailed rims set with little shields symbolising the wearer's jurisdiction over the granting of arms. No other examples of this form of crown are known, though down to the beginning of the seventeenth century illustrations of crowns worn by kings of arms at different dates are plentiful and show them to have been of various shapes with fleurons, trefoils, points, and balls. From the time of Charles I, the crown took the form of conventional leaves set on an engrailed rim. After 1720, this rim ceased to be engrailed. The crowns of Clarenceux and Norroy are of silver-gilt; Garter's crown is of gold, and had been of that metal since shortly after 1636. The inscription round the rim reads:

'MISERERE MEI DEUS SECUNDUM MAGNAM MISERICORDIAM TUAM'
(*Psalm li, i*)

The curious may note that this was the notorious 'neck verse' of pre-Reformation days whereby murdering and thieving clerks (monastery servants, minor clergy and so on) had been able to escape just retribution in the King's courts by reciting it before the sheriff and thus, through 'benefit of clergy', getting their case transferred to the laxer bishop's court. It is not suggested that the heraldic use of this verse is other than coincidental.

Rods or Sceptres

In medieval coronations it was the sceptre rather than the crown which was regarded as the ultimate symbol of royal power. It was natural, therefore, in an age that attached great significance to outward symbolism, that some sort of rod or staff should have also been bestowed on those who were chosen to exercise some portion of the royal prerogative. From at least Tudor times a long white staff, or stave, was bestowed upon great officers of state to be carried by them on formal occasions, and formally broken across the knee when the sovereign from whom they had received their commission died, or when they were dismissed or resigned the royal service. These high officials were the Lord Treasurer, the Lord Steward, the Lord Great Chamberlain and the Earl Marshal. There has been no Lord Treasurer since the office was put into commission in 1714, but the other great officers of state still carry their white staves on occasion. The Earl Marshal, who today carries his white stave before the sovereign in the procession at the opening of Parliament, on other occasions carries a golden rod the length of a baton as the symbol of his rank and authority.

Just when the kings of arms received this privilege is uncertain. William Bruge, in his petition to Henry V, asked for a long white rod with a little banner of the arms of St George at the end 'in token of his sovereignty and government in the office of arms' (Wagner: *Heralds of England*). In the same petition Bruge asks that the other kings of arms should have 'no such rods'. This latter request is ambiguous, but Sir Anthony Wagner believes that other kings of arms may well have been granted *other types of rod or stave* before this date. Whether or not this was the case, it seems fairly clear that by Tudor times all three kings of arms had acquired rods. Sir Thomas Wriothesley, as Garter, appears to have had two rods, one black and one white. The white rod was gilded at the end and bore a small banner of St George impaling the royal arms. This is essentially Garter's badge (not the rod) today. Both white and black rod were carried in processions of the Order of the Garter, and the black rod had, and still has, its Gentleman Usher, whose office possibly predates even Garter King of Arms. This rod is borne by the Gentleman Usher in his other capacity as servant of the House of Lords when he goes to knock with it on the closed door of the Commons chamber to summon the Speaker and Members to the Lords. An early comment speaks of the white rod as signifying 'joy', and the black rod as signifying 'punishment', a reminder that medieval people loved to attach allegorical meanings to their ritual and cere-monial insignia. Another reference from Wriothesley's time speaks of Garter's rod being of silver gilded at the ends. Whether this was his white rod transformed, or whether there was one rod for Wriothesley's duties as herald of the Order of the Garter and another to mark his sovereignty over the other heralds is difficult to determine. By the end of the sixteenth century, however, Garter's rod was definitely silver-gilded at both ends and carried the badge already referred to. In the eighteenth century the rod became gold, as it remains today. The provincial kings seem to have had white rods silvered with a badge of a 'martinet' (an heraldic bird originally identical with the dove, the symbol of peace). It is possible that each herald was also given a rod, by his provincial king of arms at the ceremony of his appointment.

In 1906 every officer of arms was given a short black baton gilded at the ends and surmounted by a badge emblematic of his particular office. In 1953, for the coronation of Elizabeth II, these black rods were replaced by white 'staves' with gilt-metal handles and surmounted by blue doves set in gold coronets.

Escutcheons and Collars

From as early as 1400 it had become the custom to pin on the breasts or shoulders of newly-created heralds little metal badges engraved with the lordships they represented. These badges would be worn on those less formal occasions when the full regalia of tabard etc would be inappropriate, such as on an official journey. These escutcheons seem first to have been of silver or silver-gilt, and in England were worn on the left 'because a knight carries his shield on the left arm': not, as the Burgundian heralds did, on the right, which a Burgundian king of arms told Olivier de la Marche was the 'nobler side'. By late Tudor times the badges had become gold, and English heralds continued to wear them until about 1630. They were restored to the heralds by permission of George VI in 1950.

William Bruge's famous petition asked also for permission to wear a collar or chain, and the Stowe MS illumination shows him wearing just such a collar. At this time, and for long after, a gold collar was often the sign of wealth as well as a mark of honour. Rich London merchants wore gold chains in the days of Edward IV, and from very early times a gold chain has formed part of the regalia of mayors. (See Chapter 6, Civic Robes and Insignia.)

The Collar of 'SS' was to become the official ornament worn on state occasions by kings of arms, by lords chief justice, and the lord mayor of London. Made up of a series of the letter 'S' in gold, linked by Tudor roses with a joining clasp in the form of a portcullis, this chain is always worn round the neck and is thought to represent the House of Lancaster. The theory is that the letters 'SS' (the letter usually occurs doubled in the chain)[3] stand for 'Seneschallus'[3] which means 'Steward'. Lord High Steward of England was a title held by John of Gaunt, who was Duke of Lancaster and founder of the Lancastrian line of kings from whom Henry VII claimed descent and his right to the throne. Whether or not this theory is correct, there is no doubt that the first Tudor king revived the use of this collar after a Yorkist interlude in which a collar of 'Roses and the Sun' had been

Page 51   The Sovereign's Coronation robes

Page 52   The Coronation robe and coronet of a Duke

the official style. It should perhaps in fairness be mentioned that another theory denies political origin, holding rather that these famous letters stand for 'Sanctus Spiritus'.

The collar was not necessarily exclusive to kings of arms, lords chief justice and the lord mayor of London, and there was one famous film, in which a great deal of attention had been paid to correct historical detail, which showed sequences of two lords chancellor wearing the Collar of 'SS'. The first showed Cardinal Wolsey on his dismissal from office having the collar removed by the Duke of Norfolk,[4] the second sequence showed the Duke in a magnificent setting representing the Tudor House of Lords placing the same collar round the neck of Sir Thomas More, the new Chancellor. Unfortunately, there does not appear to be enough evidence to prove that this famous chain was at the time an integral part of the Chancellor's official insignia. Nor need the fact that Holbein's well-known portrait of More shows him wearing a Collar of 'SS' be taken as evidence of an early judicial or ministerial use, since the portrait was painted in 1527, and More did not become Chancellor until October 1529. It seems more likely that this particular collar was simply a mark of honour signifying Henry VIII's personal regard for this great man.

2 THE CORONATION: THE ROYAL ROBES AND REGALIA

Introduction

Every year when the Queen opens Parliament in state she wears a crimson state robe with long train and the Imperial State Crown. But the splendour of the full regalia and royal cloth-of-gold robes worn since ancient times by the Kings and Queens regnant of England is seen only on the rare occasion of a coronation. We shall be looking at each item of this regalia and robing to discover so far as is possible the precise significance of each; but a more important problem demands attention first. Why was coronation thought to be not merely important but absolutely necessary in Christian monarchies throughout the middle ages and for long after? There can be no doubt that in countries such as France and England the inauguration of a new monarch meant much more than an excuse for feasting and picturesque ceremonies. There was among all classes of society a deep-seated belief that the new king, whether coming to his throne by Divine right of primogeniture or by election, had neither the right nor the power to function as ruler of his subjects until he had undergone at the hands of the Church certain rites which included an anointing with oil. It was believed that the prince was not king until the holy rites had made him so. Thus Froissart, writing of Henry IV conferring the accolade of knighthood at the Tower on the very eve of his coronation, calls him not King but Duke of Lancaster. But once these rites had been performed in the presence of and with the approval of the people, the person of the King was henceforth sacred and it was an offence against God to lay profane hands on him. That is one reason why our fore-fathers made the penalties for high treason so horrible—to draw attention to the almost blasphemous nature of the crime. As late as the reign of Charles I the penalty for drawing a sword in anger in the presence of the monarch was to have that sword hand cut off. The difference in status of the prince become king before coronation and after was further underlined by the ancient tradition that required him to take up residence in the Tower of London until he was escorted to Westminster on the eve of his coronation. In the middle ages, when the political circumstances attending the demise of one monarch and the accession of another were often fraught with danger, the Tower was the safest refuge. The last monarch to observe this tradition was Charles II.

No doubt much of this belief universally held in medieval Europe had sprung from roots in a legendary past, when the King was looked on as magician, priest and a god. In Christian times the business of king-making came to be set firmly in a sacramental rite which, despite the great religious changes of the sixteenth century, has in England remained to this day fundamentally unaltered. This is an historical fact that seems to defy rational analysis. There are some who hold that a modern coronation can only be justified as a legitimate opportunity for the exhibition of national pride, while others look on such an occasion as a sinful waste of time, money and energy. The fact remains that England is, despite appearances to the contrary, still a Christian state; and if it does nothing else a coronation draws attention to the fact that her titular ruler must by law be inaugurated with Christian rites.

We shall see that the symbolism of rite and investiture in Westminster Abbey speak of the bestowing of special power delegated to the prince by God, which is called the Prerogative. But how, it may be asked, can this be justified today when the royal prerogative is, in effect, exercised by ministers responsible to an elected House of Commons? Sir Harold Nicholson in his *Monarchy* has written: 'It is the venerability and continuity of our monarchy that gives it so strong and wide a sentimental appeal'. And, he has added, 'through pageantry . . . the sovereign . . . acquires an aura of grandeur'. These thoughts are surely present and recognised if not expressed by those millions witnessing the pageantry of Accession and Coronation who *understand* that the executive government called into being by their votes draws its power to govern from that one royal source which will receive back that power and bestow it again on other governments according to the people's will. There is also such a phenomenon as a feeling of national greatness, a source of legitimate pride. Nicholson quotes Professor Black on this subject of Monarchy—'It nullifies in the ordinary subject his feeling of smallness'.

The Coronation Ceremonies

Early History

The English coronation service in a recognisable form can be traced back to the tenth century when St Dunstan, Archbishop of Canterbury, drew up a form of investiture and coronation for the Saxon King Edgar, known as 'the Peaceable', who ruled all England, and who, according to tradition, was once rowed on the river Dee at Chester by eight tributary kings or chieftains. For his service, Dunstan borrowed from the investiture rites of the Holy Roman Emperors and from those of the Byzantine Emperors of Constantinople. By Dunstan's time the empire of the West founded by Charlemagne had become German, and its emperors received two coronations—the German crown at Aachen, and the imperial crown from the Pope at Rome. The German coronation included a form of election and recognition by an assembly of the German princes. This was followed by investiture with the sword, the emblem of military supremacy; and these elements are found in the Saxon coronation. From the Byzantine rite with its elaborate Greek ceremonial, Dunstan may have borrowed investiture with ring, sceptre, rod and imperial mantle. But the central act in the king-making was anointing with oil. And because this anointing had direct Scriptural authority ('Zadok the priest and Nathan the prophet anointed Soloman King'), the ordering of the coronation became the exclusive prerogative of the Church, and of the Archbishop of Canterbury in particular.

In the centuries that followed there were only two revisions of the English coronation rite. The first, at the end of the eleventh century, was named the *Anselm Ordo* after William Rufus's archbishop who was a leading figure of reform. The next revision was in 1308 when Abbot Lytlington of Westminster headed a commission appointed to order the coronation of Edward II. At this coronation for the first time the King of England sat for his anointing and crowning in the chair made by order of his father to contain the Scottish Stone of Destiny captured from Scone Abbey by 'Great Edward'.

The Liber Regalis

This is the ancient manuscript containing the coronation Ordo of Abbot Lytlington and now in the possession of the Dean and Chapter of Westminster Abbey. It is said to date from the coronation of Richard II's consort, Anne of Bohemia, who was crowned in 1382.

The Liber Regalis was recognised as the principal authority for the order of ceremony and form of words in succeeding coronations. Those which have taken place since James II have differed only in respect of relatively minor alterations made necessary by religious and political changes since the Reformation. Our purpose being to describe the coronation ceremonies and their history, it will prove simplest to base this description on the rules and rubrics of the Liber Regalis.

1. *The Coronation must take place in Westminster Abbey*

King Edgar was crowned by St Dunstan at Bath. Later Saxon kings were crowned either at Kingston-on-Thames, in Surrey, or at Winchester, the capital of Wessex. Edward the Confessor was himself crowned at Winchester, the last English king to be crowned there. According to an old legend, the saint was visited by St Peter who commanded him to build him an abbey on the then deserted Thorney island in the Thames, west of London. This abbey, which was to be staffed by Benedictine monks, was to develop into a royal city containing not only the monastic buildings but the royal palace and courts. The abbey church was expressly designed for future coronations and was completed very shortly before the Confessor's death. He was buried in it in January 1066, and his successor Harold, the last Saxon king, was the first of the Kings of England to be crowned in it. Less than a year later William the Conqueror was King, and so important did he consider his claim to be Edward's legitimate successor that he insisted on his own coronation taking place in the same abbey. That was on Christmas Day, 1066. Since that date every English monarch except Edward V, the Prince murdered in the Tower, and Edward VIII who abdicated in 1936, has been crowned in Westminster Abbey. The original church of the abbey, as we have noted, was designed for coronations, and took the form of a central low tower over a space from which choir, transepts and nave radiated to the four points of the compass. In this central space, called 'the theatre', English kings were to be enthroned where the greatest number of persons could see them. Henry III, who built the present abbey on the site of the Confessor's church, was careful to preserve these essential features.

2. *The Coronation ceremonies must always be performed by the Archbishop of Canterbury, or in his absence by a suffragan bishop of the Province of Canterbury*

This rule recognised a privilege confirmed to the Archbishops of

Canterbury by Papal decree. In earlier days, the privilege had not always been acknowledged, and William the Conqueror, for instance, was crowned by the Archbishop of York. The reason seems to have been that Stigand, the Saxon Archbishop of Canterbury, was at the time under a Papal ban, and William was anxious that no doubts should be cast on the validity of his coronation over a people he had just conquered. Not unnaturally, future Archbishops of York continued to lay claim to act as Canterbury's deputy, and even the right to crown the Queen Consort when Canterbury was present. These claims were always resisted, and the dispute reached a climax when Henry II, in the absence of Archbishop Becket whom he had exiled to France, arranged for his eldest son to be crowned in his own lifetime by the then Archbishop of York. On receiving the news, Becket promptly excommunicated his northern colleague, and this sentence was confirmed by the Pope. The martyrdom of Becket in his own cathedral, which followed not long after, set the seal on the decision arrived at by the excommunication.

In the prevailing temper of public opinion Henry II was in no position to support the claims of York, even if he had so wished, and it was tacitly agreed that, although they had the right to be present, the Archbishops of York could have no part in the ordering of any future coronation. It was further decreed at this time that whereas they were to be as before 'Primate of England', the Archbishops of Canterbury were to be 'Primate of All England'. So it was settled, although for a few years Archbishops of York continued to dispute Canterbury's rights. By way of example we may note that at Richard I's coronation in 1189 Archbishop Baldwin of York went so far as to engage in an unseemly struggle for possession of the Archbishop's chair, but ended up by 'falling heavily on his bum', as an early monk chronicler (surely of the southern province) gleefully puts it. After this we hear no more of such arguments, northern archbishops no doubt fearing to risk the possibility of such ghastly affronts to their archiepiscopal dignity.

We may note in passing that after these events only two English sovereigns were not crowned by the Archbishop of Canterbury. One was Mary Tudor, who was crowned by her Lord Chancellor, Stephen Gardiner, Bishop of Winchester. But he was a suffragan of Canterbury, and the Archbishop was Cranmer, who had been suspended for suspected heresy. Curiously, the other case was Mary's successor, Elizabeth I, who was crowned by Bishop Oglethorpe of Carlisle in January 1558/59. He, of course, was of the northern province, but there was a valid reason—the see of Canterbury had been vacant since the death of Cardinal Pole, and the new queen had not been able to persuade any other bishop to undertake this duty because they suspected her of heresy (she was to deprive and imprison most of them a few months later).

3. *The Ceremonies of Coronation are to consist of the following parts in this order:*
   (i)   Election
   (ii)   Confirmation of Election
   (iii) The Coronation Oath
   (iv)   The Anointing
   (v)   Investiture with Robe and Mantle
   (vi)   Investiture with Regalia
   (vii) Enthronement, or Elevation
   (viii) Homage of Clergy and Nobles
   (ix)   Coronation of Queen Consort
   (x)   Coronation Mass resumed and Howselling (Communion) of King and Queen
   (xi)   Te Deum and Recessional

(i) *Election:* This ceremony, now abandoned, normally took place in Westminster Hall where the King-elect took his seat on the 'Marble Bench'. From this seat at one time the kings used to dispense justice in person, sitting in the Curia Regis or King's Court; and when the courts became separated from the Council criminal proceedings by the Crown continued to be conducted by royal judges, ie, professional lawyers, sitting on the King's Bench. But for this unique occasion the King returned to be formally acclaimed or 'elected' by the assembled bishops and nobles before proceeding to the nearby abbey for coronation. In Saxon times, election had often been a reality because primogeniture had not yet become the law, and the choice of a successor to the dead monarch rested with the Witanagemot, though their choice was restricted to members of the royal house. There continued to be some freedom of choice in Norman times, as is witnessed by the succession of William Rufus, Henry I, Stephen and John, none of whom had been direct heirs. Today the new monarch, succeeding by right of primogeniture, is formally acclaimed by the Accession Council (successor to the Witanagemot) meeting immediately after the demise of the Crown at St James's Palace. (See Prologue).

(ii) *Confirmation of Election:* The King-elect having been conducted with pomp into the abbey church, he was *presented* by the Archbishop of Canterbury to the nobility, clergy and people from the 'theatre' to the four corners of the church; and the people signified their assent by repeated cries of 'God save the King . . .'

(iii) *The Coronation Oath:* From Saxon times it had been the custom for the King-elect to make certain promises on oath before the Archbishop could begin the Mass and proceed to the sacramental part of the coronation service. The substance of this oath was to vary considerably, but in essence it was a solemn undertaking by the King to be a good lord to the chief tenants of the Crown. After Magna Carta this oath was to be more specific, binding the monarch to rule according to the established laws of the kingdom.

(iv) *The Anointing:* In Christian Europe anointing had been from earliest times regarded as the central act of the whole coronation rite. Because of the close association with the Church's sacraments which made use of consecrated oil, it was widely believed that the King himself by anointing was set apart and raised up to a position different in kind rather than in degree from that of his subjects. By solemn anointing the King's person was made sacred. It is not known when and where the custom was introduced into western Europe. The first definite mention we have of a king being anointed is that of Pepin, King of the West Franks, who was anointed in the year 751. Pepin was the father of the great Emperor Charlemagne, and like his more famous son a staunch upholder of the Papacy which he defended against the pagan Visigoths. There is no reason to suppose that Charlemagne was not anointed when he was crowned 'King of Germany' at Aachen, but it is not clear whether he received a similar blessing when Pope Leo III placed the imperial diadem on his head in St Peter's, Rome, a few years later. In 936, when the Holy Roman Empire was revived by the Emperor Otto I, that monarch was anointed at Aachen. It is also very likely that those responsible for the coronation rites of these monarchs went for authority to a far older royal line, the Greek Emperors of the East Roman Empire known as Byzantium. In England, the first recorded anointing is when Offa, king of the Midland Saxon Kingdom of Mercia, had his son hallowed thus as his successor in 785. This was the Offa who built the great dyke that still bears his name. We do not know if all the Saxon kings were anointed, but before the end of the tenth century this ceremony was taken for granted, and we are sure that St Dunstan anointed King Edgar. We know also that this archbishop saint put the consecration of the King on the same level as baptism and confirmation, and this view would have been reinforced for contemporary opinion by the fact that the oil used on this occasion was chrism and not oil of the catechumens.

To understand this it is necessary to explain that the Catholic Church has always used three kinds of oil for her sacraments, the basis of each being olive oil. Only two of these oils need concern us, and the material difference lies in the fact that in the preparation of chrism, the more important oil, a distillation of certain aromatic herbs called 'balm' is added. This is the oil used by the Church for the ordination of bishops and priests, and its use by Dunstan goes far to explain why the anointing of a king came to be regarded as a true sacrament of the Church. Medieval theology logically concluded from this that, by anointing with the oil of bishops, the king was given at least priestly status, and equal authority in Church matters with the bishops. In an age dominated politically by the struggle for supremacy between the Papacy and the sovereign state, the consequences are not hard to foretell, and it is not surprising to learn that, influenced by the reforming zeal of the eleventh-century Pope Gregory VII, the Anselm Ordo of the coronation substituted the ordinary oil of the catechumens for chrism. As if to compensate for this loss, the Ordo directed that the king should now be anointed on the hands, the shoulders, the arms, and the breast, as well as on the head. The only alteration made in the Abbot Lytlington rite was to restore the use of chrism for the head anointing, ordinary oil continuing to be used for the other anointings. And so the custom continued until the Reformation brought changes.

The last Catholic monarch to be crowned with pre-Reformation rites was Queen Mary Tudor in 1553. Because this most devout queen suspected her bishops had been contaminated by the Protestant heresy of her father's and the last reign, she insisted on chrism oil for her coronation being brought to England from Brussels (the Burgundian capital of her cousin, the Emperor Charles V). With Mary's Protestant successors, the mystical significance of anointing was deliberately suppressed, and later the Puritans wished to do away with anointing altogether. It was felt, however, that tradition and the centuries had so hallowed this ancient rite that to leave it out would imply a diminution in the authority of the monarch. It must be remembered that this was the age when the doctrine of the Divine Right of Kings was being officially encouraged. In 1689, when the coronation service received its last revision, Bishop Compton transferred all blessings, including that of the anointing oil, from sacramentals and ornaments to the monarch himself. For the last two coronations it is believed that the oil was privately blessed by the archbishop or a suffragan bishop before the public ceremonies.[1]

(v) *Investiture with Robe and Mantle:* The coronation robes and regalia will be described in detail at the end of this chapter. Their origin is unknown. We may note that there is mention of a special mantle being worn by the King at Edgar's coronation, but no details of this or of later coronations is available until the reign of Richard I, when a contemporary chronicler speaks of the royal robes being carried on a board behind the regalia in the procession into the abbey. The chronicler does not record what these robes consisted of, and we have to wait until the time of Richard II for the complete list as retailed in the Liber Regalis, which also directs that between coronations they should be kept with the regalia by the abbot and monks of Westminster. They were, presumably, stored in the Jewel Tower of the monastery. A striking feature which is noted by contemporaries is the similarity of these robes to the sacramental vestments of a bishop, eg, the Colobium Sindonis, or the Tunica, and the Stole. It is hard to resist the conclusion that these robes, which were of cloth-of-gold and ceremonially placed one by one on the anointed king, deliberately symbolised the sacramental nature of a king's consecration, as Dunstan had held.

What is less well-known is the nature of the robe which the monarch-elect wore in procession to the abbey. In modern times, and for several hundred years past, these have consisted of an under-dress of white knee-breeches, silk shirt with full sleeves, crimson and gold laced surcoat close-fitting, and crimson mantle with ermine and miniver hood and long train. On the head is worn a crimson velvet tall cap with a miniver fur base. It has been suggested that this dress symbolises the King-elect's rank as a royal duke. In earlier medieval times he may well have worn the surcoat and tunic of a knight, such as was worn by nobles when not in armour, but no evidence is available.

After the coronation ceremonies and Mass were completed, the newly-consecrated monarch was stripped of the actual coronation robes which were, as we have noted, returned to the Abbot of Westminster. He must then have been robed in more secular finery, but it is not until Richard II's time that we have any details. By this time it becomes clear that a long crimson or purple cloak with ermine hood and long train was put on the monarch. Details are given below.

(vi) *Investiture with Regalia:* After the anointing and investment with the royal robes came the conferring of the regalia at the hands of the archbishop. By the middle of the thirteenth century the order of conferring each item had been established as follows: ring, armills (bracelets), spurs, sword, St Edward's Crown, sceptre and rod. This order differs in one important respect from that of modern times in that today the crown is placed on the monarch's head last as the climax of the whole coronation ceremony. In medieval times it was believed that the climax was the solemn anointing, and the conferring of robes and regalia simply a symbolic act confirming the new status the prince had acquired. The sceptre was conferred last of all because, in medieval eyes, this was the chief symbol of kingly power, and not the crown. Visitors to the National Portrait Gallery in London may gaze on the portrait of Henry IV who holds the royal sceptre but does not wear a crown.

(vii) *Enthronement:* This was the 'lifting up' of the newly-consecrated king in the sight of his tenants-in-chief and the people, symbolic of his ascendancy over his new subjects. The ceremony seems to have had its origin in the ancient German custom of lifting up the newly-elected chief on the shields of his warriors while they acclaimed him. The Liber Regalis directs that the King, robed and invested, shall be led between two bishops (of Durham and Bath and Wells) and surrounded by the great officers of state from the coronation chair to the throne set up on a dais in the 'theatre'. There, while the drums and trumpets sound, shall he receive the homage and fealty of his chief tenants.

(viii) *Homage of Clergy and Nobles:* The assembled bishops, abbots and nobles of the realm were now required to perform homage to the King seated on his throne, while the abbey choir sang anthems from the coronation Mass. Homage was done for the feudal land tenure, and it must be remembered that bishops and monasteries held very large estates before the Reformation. Fealty was performed only by the clergy for the 'spiritualities', that is their authority to exercise their powers as bishops. The Archbishop of Canterbury, as the first subject of the King, was always the first, and he was followed by the other bishops and then the abbots. There followed the temporal peers in order of their degrees, beginning with the princes of the blood, and then the dukes (there were no dukes in England until the middle of the fourteenth century). The rubric directed that the peer should kneel at the foot of the throne and recite the following:

> 'I . . . become your liege man of life and limb, and of all
> earthly worship and faith, all truly bear unto you, to live
> and die with you against all manner of folk. God so help
> me and All-hallows.'

Immediately after doing homage, the peer was directed to ascend the steps of the throne, kiss the monarch on the cheek, and touch the crown with his fingers. In modern times kissing the cheek is restricted to princes of the blood, and at the coronations in 1937 and in 1953 only the senior peer of each degree and the Archbishop of Canterbury, on behalf of all the bishops, performed homage. In medieval times, of course, the number of temporal peers seldom exceeded thirty or forty, whereas in 1953 there were over nine hundred!

(ix) *Coronation of the Queen Consort:* It was at this point in the rite that the wife of the King was anointed and crowned. The ceremony seems to have been peculiar to England. In France, for example, the wife of the monarch took no part in the coronation ceremonies. The English queen was anointed with ordinary oil on the head and breast only, and was then invested with a royal purple robe and crowned before receiving a sceptre and a rod. Supported by two bishops, she was then conducted to her throne in the theatre, which was placed one step lower than that of the King. She was directed to make an obeisance to the King as she passed in front of his throne.

(x) *The Offertory of the Coronation Mass, and the Howselling of the King and Queen:* At the offertory of the Mass, the King now offered an oblation of bread to be laid on 'the paten of St Edward's chalice'. At the same time he offered 'a mark of gold'. While the *Agnus Dei* was being sung after the consecration, the archbishop carried the Pax to the King and the Queen, who then kissed it. This Pax was a small gold disc used in the ceremony of the Kiss of Peace. Then, proceeding to the high altar, the King and Queen were directed to prostrate themselves full length for the *Confiteor* and Absolution. After this they were howselled (made their communion), while two bishops held a long white silk cloth before them. Finally, the archbishop received from them their crowns which he reverently placed on the altar.

The medieval rite apparently required the monarch and his wife to receive communion crowned, and not bareheaded, as is the modern custom. We do not know for sure what was done with their crowns while they lay prostrate for the *Confiteor* but, presumably, they were temporarily removed to be held with rods and sceptres by the attendant bishops.

(xi) *Te Deum and Recessional*: Mass being ended, the King and Queen retired to a place prepared behind the high altar to break their fast briefly while the Lord Great Chamberlain received from them the rest of the regalia. This was then conveyed to the Abbot of Westminster who laid them, together with the crowns, on the altar for later return to the Jewel Tower. Then, while the choir sang the *Te Deum*, the King and Queen retired to St. Edward's shrine to pray before the relics of the Confessor who had remained the patron saint of the Kings of England after St George had displaced him in 1350 as principal patron of England. Their prayer ended, and the King having been arrayed in surcoat and mantle with train of purple velvet and ermine-trimmed hood of estate, he and the Queen, wearing their second crowns and holding sceptres, accompanied by clergy, the great officers of state and preceded by the heralds, walked in procession the length of the abbey church to the sound of trumpets, organ and drums. And all the while the abbey bells rang a joyous peal, and the people inside and outside signified their joyous approval with repeated huzzas.

The King, incidentally, would now have been wearing his second crown over a white linen coif wrapped around his head. This coif was to protect the holy oil of anointing, and would not be removed for eight days. On the eighth, or octave day, two bishops would visit the palace and, after removing the coif, would solemnly wash the King's head with hot water.

The Coronation Banquet

The great banquet in Westminster Hall that followed the coronation of an English king was always much more than an excuse for celebrating a great occasion. It seems likely that all or most of the Saxon kings held banquets, and certainly from Norman times down to George IV in 1821 every coronation has been followed by this splendid feast. The next monarch, William IV, abandoned the practice on grounds of economy, and it has not been revived since. The custom was an ancient one already well-established in Germany by Dunstan's day, and its importance lay in the opportunity it afforded for the feudal lords to perform certain duties and to receive rewards from their king. These duties included the offering of a cup, the presentation of certain dishes, the holding of a sword, and so forth; and the right to perform them was so eagerly sought after that there was frequently heated argument, not always settled amicably. This is understandable when it is remembered that such personal service to the new monarch was likely to be rewarded not only by material gifts, but by the grant of ministerial office.

In England, a small number of nobles in charge of the various domestic arrangements of the king's household naturally came to play an important part in these proceedings. When, in the twelfth century, certain officials separated from the royal household to head departments of state, they did not cease to consider themselves members of the domestic household but, as great officers of state, claimed the right to perform at a coronation duties which their humbler predecessors had undertaken as a matter of course daily. Thus, the old steward of the household has become the Lord High Steward appointed to preside over the High Court of Parliament, the overseer of the royal chamber has become the Lord Great Chamberlain, the constable in charge of the royal stables and horses the Lord High Constable, and so forth. These men had little difficulty in maintaining their privileged positions; but kings liked to reward faithful service and loyalty, especially on the occasion of a coronation. Thus, with the passage of time there was a tendency to regard privileges once granted as hereditary, and, since there had been no coronation for fifty years, it is not surprising to learn that when Richard II came to the throne in 1377 a Coronation Court of Claims was set up to determine the validity of the many claims then made.

This first Court of Claims was presided over by John of Gaunt in his capacity as Lord Steward, and from that time on such a court has been assembled under the Lord Steward of the day before every coronation, though it is not certain that he has always presided in person. By the eighteenth century, the court had become a commission of the Privy

Council, possibly because many members of the old Steward's court were Jacobites and therefore, from the Whig government's point of view, untrustworthy. After the coronation of George IV there has always been inserted in the royal warrant calling the commission into existence a clause 'excepting those ceremonies formerly rendered the sovereign in Westminster Hall'.

Thanks to television and press photography, most people who never manage to get near Westminster Abbey have some idea of the magnificence of an actual coronation service; but the splendours once seen in Westminster Hall are lost for ever, and we have to rely on a few old prints and odd passages from a handful of writers who were privileged to witness that scene. Horace Walpole has described the banquet of George III, which he himself witnessed, and Walter Scott wrote a description of that same banquet in *Red Gauntlet*. Although Scott could not himself have been present, he knew personally many people who were. Let us, therefore, end this chapter with an imaginative description based on these sources of the scene in William Rufus's great hall transformed for a coronation banquet.

We look down from galleries specially erected to accommodate the wives of peers and other special guests. High above us, nearly three thousand wax candles grouped in great clusters beneath Richard II's hammer-beam roof cast their golden glow over a scene of magnificence and beauty. Seated at long, damask-covered refectory tables running the length of the hall is a great company of the highest and the noblest in the land, all clothed in brilliant robes and liveries of state: peers of the realm in crimson and miniver, the lords spiritual in white lawn and black velvet, the lord mayor and aldermen, and a host of knights and gentlemen arrayed in the colours of the rainbow. The scene is one of animation and warmth as scarlet-clad pages of honour and servants in livery move silently among this great assembly filling the silver cups and Venetian glasses of their masters. Down the length of the hall and at the great end doors stand the King's Bodyguard of the Yeomen of the Guard in their Tudor liveries of scarlet, black and gold. The candlelight catches the bright blades of their tall partisans. There is so much movement and colour that the eye is both dazzled and bewildered. But it is not on this scene that all eyes most often rest. Sooner or later the gaze is turned to the far end of the hall where, high on a dais under a great cloth of estate, sits the newly-consecrated monarch in whose honour this great feast is being held. Arrayed in imperial purple and ermine, and with the golden crown on his head, he looks what he is from this day forward until the day he dies, the embodiment of power and majesty. Ranged round him and his consort are the great officers of state, Lord Steward, Chief Butler, Great Chamberlain, and so on. Ranged also round the dais stand the heralds of England, while behind the sovereign with drawn swords stand the Gentlemen Pensioners, that bodyguard which is closest to the King. (In the nineteenth century this body was transformed into the Honourable Corps of Gentlemen-at-Arms).

The banquet itself is of three courses, which to modern eyes seems modest enough. In medieval times, however, a 'course' constituted a banquet in itself, with as many as thirty dishes of a great variety of fish, meat, game and pastry. No doubt many of the hot dishes arrive at the tables in a somewhat congealed condition as a result of their long journey from kitchen to hall, but nobody seems to mind. To the spectators in the galleries the sight and the aroma of so much food and drink must have been tantalising in the extreme. Some thoughtful persons have brought their own food with them, while others, notably peeresses, are lowering baskets by ropes to the floor of the hall where they are filled by the pages of their husbands with good things to be drawn up to the galleries. Each course is introduced by ceremony. Preceded by a fanfare and the sound of beating drums, the silver and gold dishes are carried the length of the hall by the Knights of the Bath in their crimson mantles, the Lord Steward and High Constable leading the procession on horseback. At the end of the first course comes what is perhaps the most magnificent moment of all the long feast.

The trumpets sound again. The great end doors are flung wide, and in rides the King's Champion splendidly arrayed in a full suit of the King's solid plate armour with bright plumed crest proudly waving above his helm. This is Mr Dymoke, Lord of the Manor of Scrivelsby in the county of Lincolnshire, exercising the hereditary privilege his ancestors have possessed since the reign of Edward II. He is mounted on a gaily caparisoned destrier, and on either side ride the Lord High Steward and the Lord High Constable in their coronation robes and with golden coronets on their brows. (See colour illustration, p. 34.) Before them go two trumpeters with the Dymoke arms blazoned on their trumpet banners, and the sergeant-trumpeter with his mace on his shoulder. There follow two esquires richly habited, one carrying the Champion's lance and the other his shield. Immediately preceeding him walks Garter King of Arms carrying a scroll. Inside the

Page 69   A Duke's Parliamentary robe

Page 70   The Court of the Exchequer, fifteenth century

doors the procession halts, and once again trumpets sound. In the silence that descends on all that vast company clearly fall the words of the challenge proclaimed by Garter:

> If any person of what degree soever, high or low, shall deny or gainsay, Our Sovereign Lord King . . ., King of England, France and Ireland, Duke of Normandy and Acquitane, . . . next heir to Sovereign Lord King . . ., the last king deceased, to be the right heir to the imperial crown of the realm, or that he ought not to enjoy the same; here is his champion who saith that he lyeth, and is a false traitor, being ready in person to combat with him; and in this quarrel will adventure his life against him, on what day soever shall be appointed.

At this point the Champion throws down his gauntlet on to the stone floor, whence after a little time it is returned to him by the herald. Twice more the trumpets sound and twice the challenge is repeated up the centre of the hall, until the procession arrives at the foot of the royal dais. The King now rises in his seat to drink his Champion's health. The gold cup from which he drank is then carried to the Champion who in turn drinks the health of the King. For the last time the trumpets sound, then, holding the golden cup on which has been replaced its elaborately carved cover, Mr Dymoke backs his horse away from the dais and, attended as before, rides out of Westminster Hall to the thunderous applause of the coronation guests. Two more courses follow and further acts of feudal service are performed, and so the long banquet comes at last to its end.

One final note: in all the long history of the coronation banquet there has been only one recorded instance of the Champion's gage being picked up after it had been flung down in challenge. At George III's banquet in 1761, the last but one ever to be held, a little old lady who somehow had found her way on to the floor of Westminster Hall picked up the gauntlet before anyone could stop her. Gravely she handed it back to the Champion, saying it was a great pity 'that so fine a gentleman should lose his glove'. Was she really what she seemed to be? Legend, supported by Sir Walter Scott, has it that actually present at this banquet, though secretly, was Prince Charles Edward Stuart who, only sixteen years before, had so nearly regained the throne of his ancestors. We shall never know if beneath the old lady's dress was the only man who had some right to return the Champion's challenge.

The Sovereign's Coronation Robes
(In order of vesting)

The Colobium Sindonis: A sleeveless, long, white linen robe open at the side, and edged all round with lace. It is gathered in at the waist by a linen girdle. Its striking resemblance to the alb worn by a bishop or priest celebrating Mass suggests an origin in the days when anointing was believed to confer priestly status on the King.

The Dalmatic (Supertunica): Made of cloth-of-gold with short, wide sleeves, the dalmatic bears a woven pattern of green palm leaves between pink roses, green shamrocks and purple thistles. It is lined with rose-coloured silk.

The name is derived from 'Dalmatia', whose national dress this garment seems to have been. This part of the world (Yugoslavia today) was once within the Byzantine empire, whose emperors wore jewelled dalmatics on state occasions. Then, from being an official robe worn by consuls and other Roman officials, its use passed to the Roman Catholic Church, whose bishops wore it over the alb and beneath the cope or chasuble.

The Stole: A band of cloth-of-gold lined with rose-coloured silk some 5ft long. At either end is set a panel embroidered with the red cross of St George on a silver ground. The stole is fringed at each end.

In the Roman Catholic Church, the stole is worn as the emblem of authority; bishops wear it round the neck hanging down in front uncrossed, while priests wear it crossed over in front for celebrating Mass. In both cases the stole is worn over the alb but under the dalmatic and chasuble. The kings at their coronations wear the stole as a bishop, but over the dalmatic. The word is derived from the Latin 'stola', the outer garment worn in the early Roman empire by ladies of the noble class.

The Pall or Pallium (Imperial Mantle): Made of cloth-of-gold worked in a pattern of silver coronets, fleurs-de-lys, green leaves, shamrocks, purple thistles, and silver eagles, the pall is very similar in shape to a bishop's cope; the significant difference being that whereas a cope is rounded at the bottom, the pall has four corners which are probably meant to represent the four corners of empire. The lining is

The Imperial Robe of Royal Purple

rose-coloured silk. It is the final robe to be placed on the newly-consecrated monarch.

The royal robes are worn only once in the lifetime of the sovereign, at the coronation. In medieval times, between one coronation and the next, they remained in the custody of the Abbot of Westminster, stored with the regalia in the Jewel Tower. The present robes are not the original. At one time it was the custom to weave new ones when the old became frayed. In this century until recently they were kept at the headquarters of the Royal School of Needlework, but today they are lodged with the regalia in the Tower of London where they may be inspected by the public. (See colour illustration, p. 51.)

The Imperial and other Robes of the Sovereign

The Imperial Robe of Royal Purple: This robe is worn by the sovereign after being crowned for the procession out of the abbey and for the ensuing royal progress. Of purple velvet, lined and edged with miniver and ermine tails, it has a miniver and ermine hood, and a gold-embroided long train.

The colour purple, it is thought, symbolises the imperial purple of the Roman Caesars which was later adopted by the Byzantine emperors and possibly by the Holy Roman emperors of medieval times (Charlemagne wore the chalmys and sandals of a Roman noble for his coronation).

The Crimson Parliamentary Robe, or Robe of State: This is the robe worn by the sovereign-elect in his progress to the abbey before coronation. It is also the robe worn for state openings of Parliament. Made of crimson velvet and embellished with gold lace, the robe is miniver-lined and edged, and has a long train.

There exist today separate purple and royal crimson robes for a king or a queen. Her present Majesty's robe was made for Queen Victoria. The King's robe does not predate the nineteenth century, but it is certain that similar robes of purple or crimson velvet, lined and edged with miniver and ermine, were worn by sovereigns at least as far back as the fifteenth century on similar occasions.

The Cap of Maintenance: Made of crimson velvet lined and edged with miniver, the cap is worn once by a male sovereign on his progress to the abbey for coronation. It is not worn by a queen regnant but

The Cap of Maintenance

carried before her. It is removed from the male sovereign's head just before the anointing.

This, or another 'cap of maintenance', is also carried by a specially-chosen peer before the sovereign on a short baton at the opening of Parliament. The peer with the cap stands on the steps of the throne at the sovereign's right, while the peer carrying the Sword of State stands at his left hand.

The origin of this cap is ancient but obscure. It is known that Pope Leo X presented Henry VIII with a 'cap of maintenance' to signify his appreciation of the Tudor king as a champion of religious orthodoxy at a time when the Church was beginning to be assailed by the onslaught of the Lutheran heresy. This particular cap was presented to the King at a service at St Paul's Cathedral in London by the Papal nuncio. It was apparently symbolic and not intended to be worn; but the King placed it on his head only to find it was too large and came down over one ear!

The Royal Regalia

The regalia proper consists of those emblems with which the sovereign is actually invested at coronation. There are, however, two other groups of ornaments—those pertaining to the Church and clergy, and those pertaining to the nobles.

The Sovereign's Regalia

The Ring: A sapphire and ruby cross of St George set in fine gold, the ring signifies the wedding of the monarch to his people, and his defence of the freedom of the Church. The sovereign is still 'Defender of the Faith', although that faith is no longer the Roman Catholic one. Placing this ring on the sovereign's fourth finger of the right hand, the archbishop says: 'Receive the ring of kingly dignity and the seal of Catholic Faith; and as you are this day consecrated to be our Head and Prince, so may you continue steadfastly as the Defender of Christ's Religion . . .'.

A new ring had customarily been made for each coronation, the old one being broken up on the death of the former monarch. In modern times this has not been done, the old ring after necessary alteration of size serving for the next coronation.

The Armills (Bracelets): These bracelets of unknown origin are of solid gold and are worn one on each wrist. They were not conferred after the coronation of James II until they were restored to the investiture for the coronation of Elizabeth II. The words of delivery are: 'Receive the bracelets of sincerity and wisdom, both for tokens of the Lord's protection embracing you on every side; and also for symbols and pledges of that bond which unites you with your people . . . .'

(Left) The Sovereign's Coronation Ring; (right) one of the two Armills, or Bracelets, of the Royal Regalia

The Golden Spurs: Known as 'St George's Spurs', these are of solid gold with gold-embroidered crimson velvet straps. They represent knighthood and chivalry. The sovereign is head of all orders of knighthood, and this bestowal of spurs formed an essential part of the medieval making of a knight. (See Chapter 5, on Knighthood.)

The modern custom at coronations is to touch the King's heels with the Golden Spurs and return them to the altar. A Queen regnant touches them only.

The Golden Spurs, known as 'St George's Spurs'

The Jewelled Sword of State: This sword is the most magnificent of all those carried at the coronation. Both hilt and scabbard are elaborately encrusted with gold tracing and precious stones. The present jewelled sword was made for the coronation of George IV.

After it has been laid on the altar the sword is brought to the King and girded on him with these words, spoken by the archbishop: 'Receive this kingly sword, brought now from the Altar of God, and delivered to you by the hands of us the bishops and servants of God, though unworthy. With this sword do justice, stop the growth of iniquity, protect the Holy Church of God, help and defend widows and orphans . . .'.

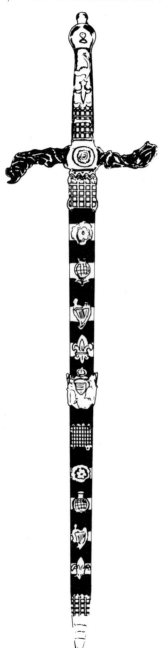

The Jewelled Sword of State

The sword is then ungirded and redeemed 'for one hundred shillings' by the lord who has hitherto carried the Sword of State. For the rest of the coronation this same lord carries the Jewelled Sword before the sovereign, while the Sword of State is laid up in St Edward's Chapel behind the high altar. The sword is not girded on a Queen regnant; she touches it only.

St Edward's Crown: This crown of solid gold set with precious stones is worn on this one occasion only in the lifetime of the sovereign. The present crown was made by Sir Robert Vyner, goldsmith, and later Lord Mayor of London, for the coronation of Charles II, most of the earlier regalia having been melted down and broken up by the Com-

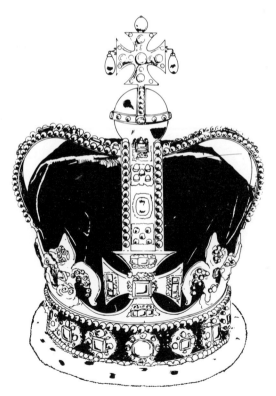

St Edward's Crown

monwealth government. It is thought that it was modelled on the old St Edward's Crown with its four imperial arches which, however, were not then depressed as they are today. Sir George Bellew, formerly Garter King of Arms, has put forward the interesting theory that the modern crown may, in fact, be made in part from gold melted down from the medieval crown.

No words are spoken in bestowing the crown, but the medieval rite had a blessing of it, and Bishop Compton inserted a blessing of the crowned monarch at this point of the rite. After James II, the order of the rite was altered so that, as today, the crowning comes last, and, as the rubric directs, 'the great guns are shot off, the assembled people make acclamation with repeated cries of 'God Save King . . .' and the peers put on their coronets'.

St Edward's Staff: Symbolically, this is a staff to guide the King's steps. It is made of gold, but has a steel tip, and is 4ft 7½in long. It was placed in the sovereign's hands at this point of the rite. He then gave it to some lord whom he wished to favour to carry before him. St Edward's Staff is no longer delivered to the monarch, but is carried in the procession.

The Royal Sceptre with Cross: As has already been mentioned, the Royal Sceptre is the ultimate symbol of kingly authority and, with the Second Sceptre or Rod, is the last of the regalia to be conferred on the newly-consecrated monarch in the old rite. The words of delivery are: 'Receive the Royal Sceptre, the ensign of kingly power and justice'.

The sceptre is made of gold, and since the reign of Edward VII has, mounted beneath the cross, the largest portion of the Cullinan diamond weighing 500 carats. From very ancient days the rod or sceptre has signified authority and power. King Ahasuerus the Persian, the Scriptures record, stretched out the golden sceptre to Esther as a sign of grace and favour. Many Syrian, Persian and Egyptian monarchs are depicted in sculpture holding rods. The rod of Moses and Aaron signified the possession of miraculous powers.

The Sceptre (or Rod) with Dove: This rod is also of gold, but is surmounted by a gold and white enamel dove signifying the Holy Ghost. It is delivered as 'The rod of equity and mercy'.

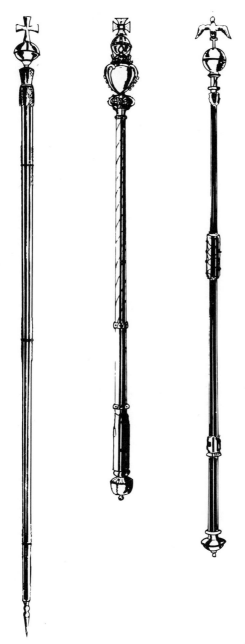

(Left) St Edward's Staff; (centre) the Royal Sceptre with Cross; (right) the Sceptre (or Rod) with Dove

There remain two emblems which, properly speaking, are not part of the royal insignia as they are not essential to the ritual of king-making. Nevertheless, the first at any rate has great significance in the royal symbolism of western Europe of the middle ages. These emblems are, respectively, the Orb, and the Second Crown.

The Orb with Cross: A very ancient symbol of royalty, this is a golden ball surrounded by a heavily-jewelled metal band from which springs a similarly jewelled arch with a cross at the apex. Its appearance in the English coronation rite was comparatively late, and the delivery has occupied more than one position. Today, it is presented after delivery of Spurs and Sword and before the Ring, but has to be surrendered almost immediately for the delivery of those greater symbols of power, the Royal Sceptres. The Orb is delivered a second time to the sovereign after the coronation in St Edward's Chapel with the Second Crown for the procession out of the abbey.

In earlier times, the Orb was carried by the sovereign on a number of other occasions during the reign, such as a state opening of Parliament, a prorogation, or on any occasion when the king was present in

The Orb with Cross

State. A well-known contemporary print shows Queen Elizabeth I before Parliament, seated on the throne and holding the Orb in one hand and the Sceptre in the other. Whether or not there is any constitutional significance in the modern omission of these emblems of royalty before Parliament, it seems a pity that the monarch could not at least enter the Lords' chamber carrying them, even if she has to surrender them in order to hold the government speech she has to read. Perhaps constitutional proprieties might be preserved if, before receiving from the Lord Chancellor the Gracious Speech, the monarch surrendered these insignia to ministers of the Crown.

Signifying the dominion of the Cross over the world, the Orb was part of the regalia of the medieval Holy Roman emperors—a statue of Charlemagne, now thought to be near contemporary, shows him mounted on horseback, a sword in one hand and an orb in the other. Similarly depicted in an illumination is the Emperor Otto III. No doubt this emblem helped to give visual expression to that world dominion the Christian emperors then claimed.

The Second Crown: The English coronation rite provided for a Second Crown, in medieval times less magnificent than St Edward's Crown and possibly without imperial arches. This crown was to be placed on the King's head after the coronation rite in St Edward's Chapel, and worn by him for the procession out of the abbey and for the ensuing coronation banquet. A 'second crown' was always worn by English kings on certain important occasions. One reason may have been that St Edward's Crown was considered too heavy for comfort. Another almost certainly was that the coronation crown was by ancient tradition in the keeping of the abbot and monks of Westminster, and would not lightly be surrendered by them for ceremonies outside their jurisdiction; in this, no doubt, they would be supported by the Church. William the Conqueror, we are told, wore his crown when he met the great Norman council of barons three times a year, at the feasts of Easter, Whitsun and Christmas, and the custom persisted through the reigns of his successors. Throughout the middle ages there must have been a number of occasions—meetings of Parliament, the successor to the Great Council, processions and services of thanksgiving for victories, and so on—when the need to impress visually a simple populace made it advisable to wear this obvious symbol of kingship. Today, the last of the old Christian monarchies, the United Kingdom constitution and custom demand that the sovereign wear the crown

The Imperial State Crown

to open Parliament. This diadem worn by Elizabeth II is known as the Imperial State Crown which was made for Queen Victoria's coronation in 1838. It is, in fact, much more splendidly jewelled than St Edward's Crown, and in spite of its late origin contains some historic gems: the great 'ruby' reputed to have been worn by Henry V at Agincourt, and which may have belonged even earlier to the Black Prince, and pearls which undoubtedly belonged to Elizabeth I, since she is seen wearing them in the famous Armada portrait in the National Portrait Gallery.

In addition to this second crown, there must have been other diadems made to suit the particular taste of individual monarchs. These would be little more than gold circlets, and have been well illustrated in illumination and heraldry. Such circlets would, for example, have been worn by warrior kings over their helmets to distinguish them in battle. Of such a type of 'crown' must have been the gold circlet that rolled from the head of Richard III at Bosworth, to be found in a hawthorn bush by Lord Stanley, who placed it on the head of the victorious Henry Tudor.

The crowns worn by Queens Consort seem to have been specially made for each such consort, and may have been broken up at death. The Crown Jewels today include crowns made for the late Queens Alexandra and Mary.

The Regalia of the Church

These are the emblems of coronation more properly to be associated with the sacramental side, and which are handled by the clergy alone. They are, nevertheless, part of the Royal Regalia, and were kept in the Abbey Jewel Tower with the rest. Today, they are lodged in the Tower of London.

The Pax: This was the gold disc to which was fitted a silver-gilt handle. It was presented to the King and Consort to kiss at that part of the Mass where the rubric directs the kiss of peace be given. It has not been used since the Reformation, and did not survive the Commonwealth.

The Chalice and Paten: These are the essential vessels without which no Mass can be celebrated. Those used for coronation Masses are likely to have been of great magnificence and made of gold encrusted with many jewels. Although medieval coronation chalice and paten very likely continued in use after the Reformation, because the abbey as a royal foundation was preserved after the monastic dissolution, there can be little doubt that they were destroyed with the rest of the regalia by the Commonwealth government. The vessels used today were made, like the rest, for the coronation of Charles II, and are of gold. They are carried into the abbey in the coronation procession by the clergy.

The Ampulla and Anointing Spoon: These are the most interesting items of the Royal Regalia, and the most historic. The present Ampulla and Spoon almost certainly predate the Commonwealth, and although at one time repairs must have been carried out they may well be the actual medieval vessels.

(Left) The Anointing Spoon of silver-gilt; (right) the golden Ampulla

The **Ampulla** is a hollow vessel of solid gold in the form of an eagle and weighs 10 oz. It holds six ounces of oil, which is poured through the beak, the eagle form of the vessel being intended to symbolise imperial dominion.

The **Spoon** is of silver-gilt and is used by the archbishop to convey the sacred oil to the parts of the monarch's body to be anointed. It is thought that the Spoon is of even older date than the Ampulla.

Originally, as we have noted, two oils were used in the coronation rite, so that, almost certainly, there must once have been two ampullas. No trace, however, remains of a second one.

Page 87   The Sovereign's robes of the Most Noble Order of the Garter

Page 88   The Lord Mayor of London's crimson velvet reception robe

The Regalia of the Nobles

This consists of the various swords carried in the coronation procession by the great officers of state (St Edward's Staff may well come under this heading as it is no longer an emblem of the investiture). The sword was one of the most primitive emblems of sovereignty, and in that prototype of early Christian kingship, the Holy Roman Empire, the emperors are often depicted with a sword in one hand and an orb in the other. The Norman and early Plantagenet Kings of England were invested as Dukes of Normandy and Acquitaine with a sword according to the already ancient tradition of those independent duchies. Medieval royal seals, too, represent the monarch with this emblem, and as late as the early sixteenth century a portrait of Henry VIII shows him crowned and enthroned, holding a sword rather than a sceptre. Signifying military power and supreme authority over national levies and feudal array, it is not difficult to understand why this emblem holds such an important place in these ceremonies. Nor is it difficult to appreciate why the duty of carrying a sword before the sovereign on public occasions was accounted an honour and a privilege eagerly sought after.

In England there are, excluding the sovereign's own Jewelled Sword, four state swords.

The Sword of State: A two-handed sword and the largest in the regalia. Like the other swords it was formerly carried unsheathed, but in modern times is borne in its richly jewelled scabbard. This Sword of State in former times was always carried by the Lord High Steward, the first of the great officers of state and a nobleman in the highest confidence of the monarch. Today, it is the only one of the four seen outside a coronation, being carried before the sovereign at the state opening of Parliament.

The Sword of Justice to the Spirituality: This sword symbolises the promise of the King to protect the privileges of the Church, a very important consideration in early medieval times when relations between Plantagenet kings and the all-powerful Catholic Church were often less than cordial. It might seem fitting that this sword should be carried by a bishop; but canon law denied clerics the right to carry sharp weapons which might shed blood (bishops did take part in battle, but carried clubs which, presumably caused only lumps!) This sword is, therefore, borne in the procession by a temporal peer.

The Sword of Justice to the Spirituality

The Sword of Justice to the Temporality: Identical with the Sword of Justice to the Spirituality. This is especially the sword of the nobles, since it symbolised the King's promise to respect the rights and the privileges of this class of society.

The Curtana, or Sword of Mercy: This sword differs from the other three in that it has a blunted end which symbolises the adage that 'Justice be tempered with Mercy'.

Ecclesiastical Note

It is no part of this book to enter into a discussion on the robes and ornaments of the clergy. It is sufficient to say that these would be those commonly obtaining at any one period for High Mass in the presence of a bishop. Before the Reformation, the rules and regulations were laid down in the Church manual known as the Pontifical, but there were local variations until the rite and ceremony used in the greater part of southern England, known as the Sarum rite, came to be adopted all over England shortly before the Reformation changed everything.

For a coronation, obviously the very best vestments would be used, but the individual articles of apparel were the same as for all High Masses:

Archbishop: white alb and stole, a jewelled mitre on the head, tunicle and dalmatic worn under chasuble and the Papal legate's pallium worn overall. In the later middle ages at any rate, jewelled gloves would be worn with the episcopal ring worn over the glove. Before the archbishop would be borne by a chaplain at all times the Metropolitan cross.

Assistant Bishops: white alb, open stole and cope, mitre.

Deacon and Sub-Deacon of the Mass: white alb; deacon only, a stole worn crossed over left shoulder. Dalmatics. These offices would, in pre-Reformation times, be filled by priest monks of Westminster.

Abbot of Westminster: He would have worn for this special occasion the vestments of a bishop, including the mitre. This, with a pastoral staff, was a privilege granted to abbots of the greater monasteries on special occasions.

3· ROBES AND CORONETS OF THE PEERS

The House of Lords : Historical Note

Before describing the origin and history of robes, coronets and ancient ceremonies of the peers of the realm, a brief look must be taken at the peers themselves.

At the present time all peers being of age and not debarred by age, mental deficiency or express exclusion, are entitled to an individual writ of summons issued by the Chancellor under the Great Seal of the Realm to attend Parliament, there to advise the monarch on the government of the realm. When assembled with the two archbishops and the diocesan bishops qualified for writs, they are collectively known as the 'House of Lords', a title not in use before the reign of Henry VIII. Until 1911 the House of Lords was in constitutional theory equal in authority with the House of Commons, saving only that, since the reign of Henry IV, the Commons had possessed the sole power to introduce money bills into Parliament, or to withhold such supplies. In practice, the Lords had rarely attempted to amend or even hold up the passing of any such financial measure, though they could in theory do just that. It was the action of the Lords in the Budget debates of 1909, when they threw out the Finance Bill of that year, that resulted in the legislation of 1911, making it impossible for them in future to do more than delay the passage of any bill coming from the Commons. At the same time all power to discuss and delay financial matters was taken away from them. Amendments in the form of a new Parliament Act in 1949 restricted their opportunities of delay still more.

Details of the composition of the House of Lords today have been set forth on the following page, and these may be summarised by stating that the House is made up of Lords Spiritual (the archbishops and twenty-one diocesan bishops in order of seniority) and Lords Temporal (divided into five degrees of rank: dukes, marquesses, earls, viscounts and barons).

The presiding officer is the Lord Chancellor, who combines with this office two others: he is a member of the Cabinet; and he is head of the judiciary (see Chapter 4, on Legal Robes). For some centuries the Lord Chancellor has himself been a peer, but in constitutional theory he need not be. Sir Thomas More, who was Chancellor between 1529 and 1532, presided over sittings of the Lords but could not vote in that assembly.

The House of Lords has three principal functions:
(*i*)   To debate politics and matters of national interest.
(*ii*) With the Commons, to legislate.
(*iii*) To act as the supreme court of appeal in law for the United
        Kingdom. (Since 1872 the judicial powers of the Lords have
        been limited to a small body of professional lawyers created
        life peers for that purpose.)

THE HOUSE OF LORDS: COMPOSITION

THE LORDS SPIRITUAL:
The Archbishop of Canterbury
The Archbishop of York
The Bishop of London
The Bishop of Winchester
The Bishop of Durham
Plus twenty-one diocesan bishops of
the two provinces of Canterbury and
York who are summoned to Parliament by seniority of consecration[1].

THE LORDS TEMPORAL:
Peers of England whose ancestors
received regular summons before
1707.
Peers of Great Britain who were
created between 1707 (Union with
Scotland)[2] and 1801 (Union with
Ireland).
Peers of the United Kingdom created
between 1801 and the formation of
the Irish Free State (now the Republic of Eire) in 1922[3].

LORDS OF APPEAL IN ORDINARY: By Acts of 1873 and 1876 the judicial
functions of the House of Lords as
the Supreme Court of Appeal for the
United Kingdom have been exercised, not by the whole body of peers
sitting under the Lord High Steward
as in former times, but by a small
number of Lords of Appeal in

Ordinary who are generally former High Court judges created life peers for this purpose. The Lord Chancellor may sit with these lords as a court.

LIFE TEMPORAL PEERS: Since 1945, on the advice of the Prime Minister of the day, the sovereign has created a number of life peerages. Mr Harold Wilson, Labour Prime Minister, on taking office in 1966, publicly stated that he would advise Her Majesty to create only life peers in future (except royal princes). There has been no creation above the degree of baron (for life) since 1963.

Originally, the peers were the tenants-in-chief of the King, receiving from him the greatest grants of land in return for military service and the responsibility for offering advice in Council. These were the Norman barons, and we should note that the word 'baron' has been loosely used at one time or another to describe all the tenants-in-chief; but even in Saxon times there was more than one degree of nobility. The greatest nobles in Saxon England were called 'eorls'—the origin is probably Danish—and in Edward The Confessor's day the country was divided into four great earldoms. This title, *earl*, was equivalent in rank to the Continental *count*, and we may note that the wife of an English earl is still called a countess. The Conqueror, who in his wisdom wished to maintain as far as possible the laws and customs of King Edward, insisted on bestowing this title 'earl' on the greatest of his tenants rather than the Norman-French one of 'count'. In effect, this was for some time thereafter the only degree of what we may roughly call the peerage. The less important title *baron* could be said to apply to all those Anglo-Norman tenants who, by possession of land and the favour of the King, ranked socially and politically above the mounted soldier class known as *knights*, but below the great earls. The earls attended meetings of the Great Council as of right, and as of right they had their seats in Parliament when that body came into existence before the end of the thirteenth century. The barons were summoned only by individual writ according to the King's pleasure, and they sat on a separate bench in the Parliament house. It was only gradually and late in the middle ages that they acquired the right to hereditary membership of the 'Lords', and, as we shall note, they received no special form of investiture at creation for some centuries.

During the course of the fourteenth century two further degrees of peerage were introduced into England from the Continent. These were the ranks of *duke* and *marquess*. The title 'duke' is derived from the Roman military rank of 'dux', and was bestowed on those German tribal leaders who accepted the overlordship of the early Holy Roman emperors. The word 'marquess' (spelt 'marquis' in the French form before the nineteenth century) may have been derived from the German 'margrave', the feudal title borne by those German lords whose territories, called 'marches', guarded the boundaries of the Empire. The earliest creation of a duke in England seems to have been the advancement to that rank of Richard, Earl of Cornwall, the younger brother of Henry III[5]. The first English marquess was Robert de Vere, Earl of Oxford, who was created Marquess of Dublin by his friend and patron, Richard II[6]. These creations were not followed by many others; indeed, until the end of the fourteenth century when Thomas Mowbray, Earl of Nottingham, was made Duke of Norfolk, the only dukes were royal princes, and until the middle of the sixteenth century the only English marquisate to be created was that of Thomas Grey, son of Elizabeth Woodville, consort of Edward IV, who was made Marquess of Dorset. The rank of *viscount* is not found in England until the end of the fifteenth century (as 'visconte' it was a title given in France to the eldest sons of counts).

We might here note that the number of temporal peers in voting strength of the House of Lords throughout the middle ages and for long afterwards remained very small by modern standards. In the reign of Henry VIII there were never more than fifty temporal peers, while with Henry's new ecclesiastical establishments at the Reformation and the disappearance of the abbots, the lords spiritual numbered only twenty-six, including the archbishops. Today there are over 900 temporal peers, although the vast majority never put in an appearance. The effective voting strength of the House today, except for very special occasions, is between 200 and 250.

Investiture of Peers

The custom of marking the ceremony of inauguration into office or

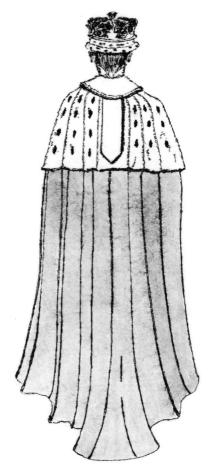

A Marquess's Coronation robe and coronet of degree

rank by conferring distinguishing ornaments is an ancient one, and we have noted the elaborate rites attending the ceremonies of king-making. Unfortunately, the ceremonies attending the creation of peers have been less well documented. We do not hear of special robes of rank until the end of the fourteenth century, but investiture with the sword is at least as old as Norman times. It is known that the Normans had a ceremony of investing their dukes with a sword in the great hall of Rouen Castle, and that this custom continued after Duke William became William I of England. Both Richard Coeur de Lion and King John were invested with swords on succeeding to kingdom and duchy. We hear also of a certain Hugh de Puiset, Bishop of Durham in Richard's reign, being similarly invested when that monarch for reasons best known to himself decided to give the good bishop the earldom of Northumberland as well. No doubt at this ceremony the prelate wore his bishop's robes and, since canon law denied him the right to put his sword afterwards to practical use, the girding-on must have been purely ceremonial and symbolic. It was during the course of the twelfth century that the investiture of earls took the form it was to retain in essentials until finally abandoned at the end of James I's reign. This form was to serve for other ranks of the peerage[7] as they were admitted in the following centuries, differences of degree being marked by the addition of certain distinguishing ornaments such as coronets and caps of estate.

Until the end of the reign of Henry V (1413-22) investiture normally took place in the presence of Parliament. After that date the ceremony was held at the King's palace. As we have noted, the earls were the first of the orders of peerage to be invested ceremonially, and that with the sword alone. With the arrival in England of the degrees of duke and marquess, a more elaborate form of ceremony was invented. The earliest account of a duke's investiture that has come down to us is that of John of Gaunt. At his investiture as Duke of Lancaster in 1362, as well as the traditional sword he received from Edward III a circlet or coronet of gold set with precious stones, a cap of estate, and a golden rod. When some years later Richard II invested Robert de Vere, Earl of Oxford, as Marquess of Dublin, he received the sword and gold circlet, but no golden rod. It is not known whether he was given a cap of estate as well, but nearly one hundred years later this mark of honour was granted to the first Marquess of Dorset. Not until 1547 was the cap bestowed on earls, and from this year dates also the custom of bestowing the coronet on earls[8]. In 1550 caps of honour were given to viscounts, but they did not receive coronets until 1604. Barons had to wait for their coronets until 1661, at the time of the coronation of Charles II.

Robes

1 Investiture Robe

In 1397 John Beaufort, Earl of Somerset, son of John of Gaunt by his third marriage, to Katherine Swynford, was clothed at his investiture

A Viscount's Coronation robe and coronet of degree

in what was called a 'vesture of honour'. It is not known what form exactly this robe took, but it seems to have been the earliest recorded example of a peer's robes. During the course of the fifteenth century 'robes of estate' were bestowed on dukes, marquesses and earls[9]. Viscounts were given the robe in the sixteenth century, but barons not until 1685. When this investiture robe came to be standardised it took the form of a crimson velvet cloak of foot length extending slightly to trail the ground at the back. It was open down the front, and was lined and edged with miniver fur. There was also a hood or cape of miniver,

A Viscount's Parliamentary robe

and later it became the custom to spot this hood with rows or 'doublets' of black ermine tails according to rank.

This investiture robe was almost certainly practically identical with the coronation robe of a peer today. It was, even in its earliest days, worn only for investitures and coronations.

2 Parliament Robe

Towards the end of this same fifteenth century appeared also another kind of ceremonial vesture for peers which came to be called the 'Parliament robe', because custom dictated that this rather than the older robe should be worn by peers attending the King in Parliament. It was a full robe of close-woven scarlet cloth of pure wool, open halfway down each side, and edged and collared with miniver. Differences in the degree of peerage were marked by the addition on right front and side to centre of back of 3in bars of miniver lined with 2in bands of gold lace. This Parliament robe, soon after its first appearance, was granted to the barons who were, as we have seen, denied the investiture robe until 1685. The pictorial roll of the royal procession at the opening of the 1511 Parliament clearly shows the peers, including barons, wearing this type of ceremonial vesture.

Ceremony of Investiture

We have already noted that the ceremony of investiture of peers fell into disuse after the reign of James I. The ceremony was one of some magnificence, and took place in the presence of the monarch. The King sat on his throne surrounded by the great officers of state. The new peer, supported on either side by two peers of his own degree acting as sponsors and preceded by Garter King of Arms carrying the patent of creation, advanced towards the throne. After the reading of the patent the new peer knelt before the King, who placed round his neck the sword attached to its belt. The coronet of degree, if there was one to be bestowed, was placed on his head, if a duke he was then handed the golden rod or verge, and finally the robe was placed around his shoulders. It is not clear from contemporary accounts at what stage in the proceedings the cap of estate was bestowed; possibly it was placed by the King on the new peer's head immediately before the coronet. This seems likely since from the beginning of the eighteenth century the custom has been to combine this cap of estate with the coronet, so that the crimson cap with attendant tassel appears as a kind of inner lining to the gold circlet, while the miniver and ermine base of the cap forms a base rim[10]. The same ceremony took place for advancements in degree of peerage as for first creations, and does not seem to have been substantially altered when investitures were transferred to the King's palace after the ceremony in the presence of Parliament was abolished. Investitures of peers were to continue for another two hundred years after 1420, though by the first decade of the seventeenth century they were often being omitted.

In passing, one might note that these ceremonial occasions were not always of a solemn nature. When Elizabeth I created Robert Dudley Earl of Leicester in 1564 as a political measure and with a view to offering him as a prospective husband for Queen Mary Stuart, who was at the time looking round for a second 'bed fellow', it is reported that she could not resist tickling the back of his neck as he knelt before her in the presence of the whole court. Dudley, of course, professed to be madly in love with Elizabeth, and she possibly with him.

When the ceremony of investiture finally lapsed, there appears to have been a strong feeling among courtiers and the peerage generally that something should take its place. It was eventually decided to introduce a special form of ceremony for new peers taking their seats in Parliament for the first time, and that this ceremony should embody some of the features of the old investiture of peers. The new ceremony then devised was essentially the same as that which is used today. It will be described in the succeeding section of this chapter on 'Ceremonies in the House of Lords'.

Notes on Robes and Ornaments

The Robe of Estate of crimson velvet, ermine and miniver fur, is practically identical with the old investiture robe, the chief difference being that in the modern robe a triangle of dark red silk is let into the centre of the ermine and miniver hood at the back. This seems to have been introduced when tye wigs became the fashion in the middle of the eighteenth century and was intended to prevent the pomade of the wig tail damaging the fur. The robe, then as now, was worn only on the occasion of a coronation.

The Coronet of Degree is also worn only on the occasion of a coronation. Peers put on their coronets immediately St Edward's Crown is placed on the head of the monarch, and continue to wear them for the rest of the coronation service and until they have left the precincts of the abbey. Peeresses put on their coronets at the moment the consort is crowned. In the case of a bachelor king, peeresses do not wear coronets, but when a queen regnant is being crowned they put them on at the same time as do the peers.

The Golden Rod of dukes disappeared with the ceremony of investiture, and has not been reintroduced, though the patent of a duke's creation still refers to the conferring of this particular ornament of rank. It may be noted that, apart from royal dukes, there have been no fresh creations of this degree since that of the dukedom of Westminster in 1874. It is, however, interesting to note that the Golden Rod still plays its part in the ceremonies attending the investiture of Princes of Wales. At the Castle of Caernarvon in 1911 for the present

The Coronation robe of a Duchess

Duke of Windsor, and more recently in 1969 at the same castle, the prince being invested was handed a golden rod or sceptre after investiture with sword and coronet, but before the robe was placed about his shoulders. This all goes to show that the ritual attending the making of Princes of Wales in modern times is markedly similar to that which attended the investiture of peers, though this has not been seen in England for three hundred and fifty years.

The coronation robes of peeresses differ from those of peers in several respects: they do not meet at the front, but are open wide the full length. They have short, close-fitting sleeves edged like the robes themselves with miniver; and—the most distinguishing mark—they have long trains, the length of which indicates the degree of rank. Colour and material are the same as for peers and, like those of their husbands, their robes are lined and edged with miniver and ermine. Coronets of peeresses are much smaller, being made to sit on top of the head, secured no doubt to the hair by special fasteners. The style of coronet indicating degree is similar to that of peers' coronets.

Ceremonies of the Lords when Robes are worn

The House of Lords has never in its long history worn robes for its sittings except in the presence of the sovereign on the throne. Today, therefore, the wearing of robes by the assembled peers is confined to the annual ceremony of the state opening of Parliament, a scene which, through the medium of television, must be familiar to millions who have never seen the interior of the Houses of Parliament. There are, however, still a number of occasions on which individual peers representing a royal commission to execute the will of the monarch wear their Parliamentary robes as an outward symbol of the royal prerogative they are called upon to exercise. This chapter will conclude with a brief description of the ceremonies attending these occasions.

Prorogation of Parliament
This is the ceremony by which a session of Parliament is brought to a close. Before the eighteenth century, when the calling of Parliaments was irregular and depended very much on the will of the monarch, he often found it useful to suspend their sitting for months and sometimes years at a time rather than to dissolve the Parliament with the chance that elections might produce a House of Commons even less amenable than the one he had. In modern times both Houses 'adjourn' for holiday recesses by their own votes, and can speedily be reassembled by order of Chancellor and Speaker if the government of the day so wishes, without reference to the sovereign. But the ancient ceremony of prorogation is still kept as a formality to end the annual session of

An Earl's Coronation robe and coronet of degree

Parliament, presumably on the grounds that this constitutional device might in special circumstances one day prove useful to a government. Queen Victoria in 1855 was the last monarch to attend a prorogation in person; since that date the ceremony has always been performed by royal commission, that is by a small number of peers—usually five— appointed by royal letters patent to act on behalf of the sovereign in his or her absence (the Lord Chancellor nearly always presides over this commission). It is thought that this procedure, which is used at all other times when the monarch is not present at an occasion demanding the exercise of the royal authority in Parliament, was invented in the sixteenth century for Henry VIII to save him the embarrassment of having to give the royal assent in person to the Act of Attainder condemning to death his own wife.

The Lords Commissioner, having taken their seats, on a long narrow bench covered with red leather and situated just below the throne, send Black Rod to summon the Commons to the Bar of the House. With the traditional bows Black Rod, preceded by the chief inspector of the Palace of Westminster police calling out: 'Make way for the Royal Commission', makes his way down the long corridor to the door of the Commons' chamber which is slammed in his face by the Sergeant-at-Arms. Black Rod gives three knocks with his rod on the door which is then opened to admit him. He advances to the foot of the table before the Speaker's chair, after having bowed three times on his way up the chamber. 'Mr Speaker', he says, 'My Lords, the Queen's Commissioners, request your presence and that of this honourable House in the House of Peers immediately.' With no further words the Speaker, who is wearing his ordinary black silk gown and full-bottomed wig, preceded by the Sergeant-at-Arms with the Commons' mace on his shoulder and Black Rod by his side, leads a procession to the Lords. He is followed by the Commons and such ministers as are present. Arrived at the Bar of the Lords, three traditional bows are made. These are returned with great dignity by the Lords Commissioner who lift their black hats and extend them at arm's length horizontal to the ground before replacing them on their heads. The royal letters patent appointing the Commissioners are read out: 'Her Majesty having thought fit not to be present . . . We have appointed our beloved cousin and councillor . . .'. The Lord Chancellor, or presiding peer, then reads the Queen's prorogation speech sitting before the throne. This speech, like the Queen's speech opening a session of Parliament, is, of course prepared by the Cabinet and reflects government comment on the record of the session now closing. Finally, the Chancellor prorogues Parliament to the agreed date (usually a few days later) and, again with the traditional bows, the Speaker followed by the 'faithful Commons' retires to his own chamber.

This procedure of summoning Commons to the Bar of the Lords is followed on every such occasion, and need not, therefore, be referred to again. It should be noted that, on arrival at the Lords' chamber, the Commons' Sergeant-at-Arms leaves the mace outside the door—this being the symbol of royal authority that may not confront the

One of the eight Royal Maces carried by
Sergeants-at-arms at Coronations and
kept in The Tower with the Crown
Jewels

sovereign or the sovereign's representatives. One final point that may be made here is that for the state opening of Parliament, when the monarch is present on the throne in person, Black Rod in addressing the Speaker substitutes the word 'commands' for 'requests' the presence of this honourable House.

Election of the Speaker

This is another ancient ceremony dating from the days when the Speaker of the Commons was as much a royal servant as presiding officer of the House. The first named Speaker was Sir Thomas Hungerford, who presided over the deliberations of the Commons of the 1372 Parliament. Although his successor, Sir Peter de la Mar, Speaker of the so-called 'Good Parliament' which impeached Alice Perrers, Edward III's mistress, and various noble oppressors of the peasantry, showed a sturdy independence of ministerial control, such impartiality did not continue, and in the late middle ages and sixteenth century, with the honourable exception of Sir Thomas More (Speaker of the 1523 Parliament), Speakers of the Commons were usually nominees of the monarch and were expected to act not only as go-betweens, but also as royal spies. Thus it came about that the sovereign insisted on approving the Commons' choice of Speaker. In the seventeenth century the constitutional struggle between King and Parliament came to a head in 1642 when Charles I violated the privilege of the Commons by entering their chamber uninvited to demand the arrest of the 'five members'. Because it established a great principle, Speaker Lentall's famous reply to the King's demand is worth re-quoting: 'Your Majesty, I have ears to hear and eyes to see only as this honourable House shall command me.'

By the end of Speaker Onslow's long tenure of office (1728-61) this principle that the Speaker of the House of Commons is removed from all royal or government control and influence was completely realised. But, as has so often happened in English history, a tradition survived to take on a new meaning. The monarch is the guardian of the liberties of the subject, and one of the ways in which an unscrupulous government, seeking to defy the electorate by unlawfully prolonging the life of a Parliament and its own majority, could be defeated, was by the monarch refusing his assent to that government's choice of Speaker. Without a lawfully-appointed Speaker the House of Commons cannot function, and it might well be that even the most unscrupulous of governments would hesitate to fly in the face of so public a condemna-

An Earl's Parliamentary robe

tion. With these facts in mind let us now examine the ceremonies attending the election of a present-day Speaker of the House of Commons.

On the first day that the newly-elected House of Commons assembles after a general election a procession, led by the Clerks of the Commons, is formed to go to the Lords where the Lords Commissioner, clothed in their scarlet and miniver robes, are waiting seated on the bench before the throne. The Lord Chancellor presiding there informs the Commons that it is the desire of Her Majesty that they should choose some proper person being a member of their House to be their Speaker. Having returned to their own chamber, one of the clerks stands up at the table before the empty Speaker's chair and, because he may not speak, points at a member who has privately been selected in advance to propose for election one of their number. The clerk then points at a second member who proceeds to second the proposal. There being no other candidate—and there rarely is—the motion is carried by acclamation.

There follows a curious little ritual: showing a traditional reluctance to accept office, the Speaker-elect is 'dragged' by his proposer and seconder, taking each an arm, to the chair. This ritual seems to have originated in the days when men were reluctant to take on an office which was almost bound to involve them in a conflict of loyalties between monarch and Commons. Standing before the chair, in which he does not sit because he is not yet Speaker, he then makes a short speech of acceptance. Usually on the following day, when the Lords Commissioner have been informed of the Commons' choice, Black Rod knocks again on the door, and another procession wends its way to the Lords' chamber. This procession is more imposing: Mr Speaker-elect, wearing black court dress with silver-buckle shoes and a tye wig but no gown—he is not yet Speaker—is preceded by Black Rod and the Commons Sergeant-at-Arms carrying the mace in the crook of his arm, while the clerks in gowns and wigs and the Commons follow two by two, Opposition members being paired with Government supporters. Standing at the Bar of the Lords the Speaker-elect informs the Lords Commissioner of the Commons' choice and requests in the name of the said Commons all the rights and privileges of that House granted in their name to his predecessors. The Lord Chancellor presiding confirms the election in the name of Her Majesty, addressing him for the first time as 'Mr Speaker', and in the Queen's name gives the traditional guarantee of the 'ancient and undoubted rights and privileges of the Commons'. The traditional three bows follow and then Speaker and Commons return to their own chamber, the Sergeant-at-Arms this time carrying the mace in its proper position on his shoulder. Mr Speaker retires, to reappear shortly afterwards attired in black silk gown and full-bottomed wig to take his seat for the first time in the Speaker's chair amid acclamation.

Introduction of a New Peer to Parliament

As has been noted, this ceremony was introduced in the seventeenth

A Baron's Coronation robe and coronet of degree

century to take the place of the discontinued ceremony of investiture of peers. It will be apparent that the modern ceremony embodies some of the features of the old one.

The House of Lords being in session, with the Lord Chancellor on the Woolsack, a small procession is formed outside the chamber. The new peer in the Parliament robe of his degree is supported on either side by two noble lords of like degree, also robed. For this occasion all three carry black cocked hats. They are preceded into the chamber by Black Rod and Garter King of Arms, the latter carrying in one hand the patent of creation of peerage, and in the other his sceptre of authority. The new peer himself carries the writ of summons. The little procession advances up the floor of the House until it fans out to stand facing the Lord Chancellor, who remains seated on the Woolsack. He wears his black gown and full-bottomed wig, surmounted on this occasion by a tricorn. Three reverences having been made to the empty throne, Garter reads the patent of creation, after which the new peer hands his writ of summons to the Chancellor. He then takes the oath of allegiance on a Testament provided by the clerk. Finally he is escorted as before to the bench of his degree in the peerage (Government or Opposition side) and takes his seat flanked by his two sponsors. All three put on their cocked hats. Three times they rise and lift their hats to the Lord Chancellor who returns the salutation with his tricorn, and the ceremony is over.

Incidentally, if the new peer is a minister, he may take his seat on the front Treasury bench, irrespective of his degree of peerage.

The Royal Assent to Bills of Parliament
This beautiful little ceremony regrettably was abolished in July 1967, ostensibly on the ground that the Commons, in the light of the pressure of modern Parliamentary business, felt they could no longer afford to waste half an hour of their valuable time every two or three months to answer a royal commission. The author was present in the gallery of the House of Lords on the very last occasion this ceremony took place. In the hope that some future government, realising the value of the symbolism which underlines the supremely important process of law-making, may one day restore it, a description is included to form a fitting conclusion to this chapter on the ceremonial of the House of Lords.

From the gallery of the Lords' chamber with its richly painted panels and stained-glass windows we looked down on the crimson leather benches ranged facing on either side of the gangway. The peers present were wearing ordinary civilian clothes. The Lord Chancellor, who a short time before had sat a solitary figure robed in black on the crimson Woolsack, had left the chamber to array himself in more magnificent robes. Extra lights now cast a soft glow on the gilded throne and on a scarlet leather-covered, long, narrow bench placed immediately below it. There was a sudden hush and the peers present rose to their feet as the five lords representing the Commission and dressed in the scarlet and miniver of Parliamentary robes silently filed in to take their seats on the bench. The Chancellor sat in the middle. With one movement they sat, and with one movement they put on their black hats. Silently they waited as Black Rod, in traditional black court dress and holding his black and gold-crested rod of office sloped on his shoulder, approached the steps of the throne. The Lord Chancellor spoke: 'Go, tell the Commons that the Lords Commissioner request the presence of their honourable House in the House of Peers immediately!'

While Black Rod was gone about his business the lords on their benches whispered together while the Lords Commissioner waited silent and motionless on their high bench. Presently and in silence Mr Speaker in long wig and black gown appeared at the Bar of the House flanked by Black Rod and the Sergeant-at-Arms without his mace. Behind ranged the members of the House of Commons. The assembly of the estates was complete—the lords spiritual represented by the presence of two white and black-robed bishops on their bench. Except for the absence of the sovereign, it was a living tableau of the scene depicted by a contemporary print of a sixteenth-century Speaker and Commons before the first Elizabeth in Parliament. Mr Speaker bowed and the salutation was returned by the Commissioners, with one graceful movement, lifting and extending their tricorns at arm's length. The Clerk of the Records rose to his feet and unfolded the large parchment sheet of the royal letters patent 'signed with Her Majesty's own hand' appointing Commissioners to pass the bills into law: 'Elizabeth II by the Grace of God . . . whereas we have thought fit not to be present . . . we have appointed to act on our behalf our dearly beloved cousin[11], and councillor . . .'. As each peer on the Commission was named he acknowledged by lifting his hat in the same beautiful salutation as before.

The reading ended, the Clerk of the Records sat down while the Clerk of the Crown and the Clerk of the Acts, rising simultaneously on either side of the Clerks' table, faced the throne. The Clerk of the Crown, after bowing to the Commission, faced the Commons to announce the title of the first bill: 'Little Trollop-on-Sea Waste Disposal Act'. The Clerk of the Acts bowed in his turn and faced the Commons and their Speaker to proclaim the old Norman-French words that make a bill the law of England: 'La Reyne le veult'. Not since Queen Anne objected to certain features of the Scottish Militia Bill of 1708 have the words, 'La Reyne s'avisera' been heard—the royal veto.

A Baron's Parliamentary robe

So the stately ceremonial proceeded, bills of national importance being treated in exactly the same way as those of only local importance. Watching from the gallery, one could not help thinking that even in these severely democratic and functional times there was something majestic and splendid about the business of law-making—the three readings and hotly-argued committee stage of most bills have occupied the mental and perhaps physical energies of hundreds of people in both Houses over a period of many weeks, and now at last, with a touch of royal splendour, the Sovereign was giving public expression to the will of her Estates. The last act was passed into law, the three traditional bows were made and Mr Speaker led his 'Faithful Commons' back to their own part of the Palace of Westminster. The Leader of the House of Lords rose to propose the adjournment, and the five Lords Commissioner rose from their bench to pass with dignity and in silence from sight. It was all over.

The Insignia and Robes of Peers

	Coronet	Coronation Robe (Doublets of ermine, ie, rows of ermine tails)	Parliament Robe (Bars of miniver and gold lace)
DUKE	Gold circlet, with 8 strawberry leaves on rim	4	4
DUCHESS	ditto	4 / 2 yd train with 5in ermine edging	—
MARQUESS	Silver-gilt circlet, 4 strawberry leaves alternate with 4 silver balls on points	$3\frac{1}{2}$	$3\frac{1}{2}$
MARCHIONESS	ditto	$3\frac{1}{2}$ / $1\frac{3}{4}$ yd train with 4in ermine edging	—
EARL	Silver - gilt circlet with 8 silver balls raised on points alternating with strawberry leaves	3	3
COUNTESS	ditto	3 / $1\frac{1}{2}$ yd train with 3in ermine edging	—
VISCOUNT	Silver - gilt circlet with 16 silver balls raised on points	$2\frac{1}{2}$	$2\frac{1}{2}$
VISCOUNTESS	ditto	$2\frac{1}{2}$ / $1\frac{1}{4}$ yd train with 2in ermine edging	—
BARON	Silver-gilt circlet with 6 silver balls set on rim	2	2

BARONESS   ditto   2
                                      1 yd train with
                                      2in ermine edging   —

Notes on Insignia and Robes of Peers

NOTE 1:   Black tricorn hats were worn by all peers with their robes
          from the end of the seventeenth century on the following
          solemn occasions in the House of Lords sitting in their
          chamber, in the royal gallery, or in Westminster Hall:
          (*i*)   Trial of Impeachment
          (*ii*) Court of the Lord Steward (trial of peers)
          (*iii*) Ceremony of introduction of a new peer
          (*iv*) Royal Commissions
          In modern times only (*iii*) and (*iv*) remain, the Lord Steward's
          Court having by implication been abolished by legislation
          in 1936, and trials of impeachment having lapsed. The last
          to be held were the trial of Warren Hastings (1788-95) and
          that of Lord Melville (1806).

          Since the beginning of the nineteenth century only the
          Lord Chancellor has worn the tricorn. All other temporal
          peers wear the black cocked hat introduced from the France
          of the Directory and made fashionable in England by the
          Duke of Wellington.

NOTE 2:   Coronets of peeresses differ from those of peers in being
          smaller in circumference, being made to fit on top of the
          head instead of encircling the brow.

NOTE 3:   Archbishops, or bishops, sitting on their bench in the Lords,
          wear purple cassock, white rochet with full sleeves and wrist
          bands, and black doctor's convocation robe and broad stole.

          In the presence of the sovereign, and on other occasions
          when temporal peers wear robes, the lords spiritual wear
          over their episcopal dress the scarlet and miniver robe of
          their degree—a duke's robe for an archbishop, a baron's
          robe for a bishop.

          In pre-Reformation times, the lords spiritual seem to have
          worn the cope and mitre of their ecclesiastical rank in the
          presence of the sovereign, while on less formal occasions
          they wore the rochet. Abbots, of course, wore the mitre
          and as an 'under dress' the habit of their order.

4 ROBES OF JUDGES, SERJEANTS AND BARRISTERS

One of the most colourful sights to be seen in England today is the opening of the assizes in a county town. The custom of holding assizes dates back at least to the reign of Henry I, but it was Henry II who decided that the future peace of the realm demanded that the royal justice should readily be available in the remotest corners of the kingdom whether the King himself was present or not. Ever since the Assize of Clarendon in 1166 the King's justices have gone forth two by two four times a year to demand in the King's name that all prisoners held in gaol should be delivered up by the sheriffs to be tried on the judge's commission of *oyer* and *terminer*, that is to answer charges of treason and felony. Sometimes, especially in civil cases, a writ of '*nisi prius*' ('unless before') directed that a jury should be empannelled at Westminster 'unless' the case had been dealt with 'before' by the judge on circuit of assize. And so because these specially trained and selected lawyers were called upon to exercise a very important part of the royal prerogative, it was natural that their arrival and departure should be accorded a respect and dignity appropriate to persons charged with dispensing justice in the King's name. And it was also natural that they should come to adopt a style of dress appropriate to that dignity.

The purpose of this chapter, therefore, is to describe the origin and the development of legal dress, and to give some account of different robes worn on different occasions. The full-bottomed wig, scarlet robe with train and full miniver fur cape and hood which Her Majesty's judges wear when they are greeted by mayor and high sheriff with a fanfare of trumpets at the opening of county assizes are discarded for the actual work of administering justice in court. Here, according to season, nature of cause and place, they may wear scarlet, violet or black robes. How this came about is, then, our immediate concern.

Old Divisions of the High Court of Justice

In the early twelfth century the administration of royal justice as distinct from that justice administered by the courts baron was still a matter for the Curia Regis, or 'Court of the King', with the King himself often presiding in person. By the middle of this century, however, two developments were in full swing: trained lawyers were taking the place of the officials of the royal household who had formerly assisted the King in Council, and separation of the department of justice from the Curia Regis was well under way. A little over a century later this process was complete, and the judges were organized in divisions according to spheres of influence. Their headquarters had become Westminster Hall, from whence they dispensed justice, and from whence certain of them, as we have seen, went forth at stated times on circuit of assize. As these 'divisions', which were to remain substantially unaltered until 1872, had some bearing on the development of judicial robes, it is necessary to describe them briefly.

Court of the Chancellor: The work of this court was to hear appeals by those of the King's subjects who thought the common law was not working fairly in their case. The Lord Chancellor presided, assisted by trained lawyers, called Masters in Chancery, who were later to be elevated to the rank of puisne judges. This court became known as the *Chancery Division*.

Court of King's Bench: The work of this court was largely concerned with criminal cases, that is prosecutions by 'the King' against the lieges for breaking the King's laws and his 'Peace'. It was so named because, before the separation of the courts from the royal household, the King himself often presided in the Curia Regis sitting on the marble bench. Now the judges of King's Bench actually took their seat in Westminster Hall on a marble bench set up at one end to represent the King's royal seat of justice.

Court of Exchequer: This division was set up to determine disputes over taxation, and its judges were called Barons of the Exchequer. The presiding judge of the division was called the Lord Chief Baron. The name 'exchequer' came from the chequer-board cloth on the table at which the clerks of Henry I's day collected the feudal taxes, piling the coin into separate squares. Among famous cases later submitted to this court's judgment were the Bate case in the reign of James I and the more famous 'Ship Money' case of Rex v John Hampden in 1636. (See colour illustration, p. 70.)

Court of Common Pleas: The judges of this court were mainly concerned with settling civil disputes between subjects. The court's work was to prove extensive, partly because possession of land being the chief form of wealth and influence throughout the middle ages there was a constant stream of acrimonious litigants, and partly because in the interests of true justice, the Crown sought to prevent alienation of property by a series of writs from the reign of Edward I onward.

Chief Justices: Each of these divisions was presided over by a chief justice. The Lord Chancellor presided over Chancery Division, and sometimes over the Court of Exchequer in the early days. But as he was also what today we should call 'prime minister', with important executive functions, unless he was himself a trained lawyer (eg Cardinal Wolsey) he usually relied on the professional advice of the other judges.

There was also a Lord Chief Justice of the King's Bench, a Lord Chief Justice of the Common Pleas and, as we have noted, a Lord Chief Baron, who came to preside over the Exchequer Court.

Prerogative Courts: We should perhaps note that from the late fifteenth century until their abolition by the Long Parliament in 1641, a number of special courts arose which were really small committees of the Privy Council appointed by the King to short-circuit long delays in the law and generally to increase the efficiency of the administration of justice. These courts, of which the more famous were Star Chamber, Court of Requests, Court of Wards, and, from the beginning of Elizabeth I's reign, the Court of High Commission, were all empowered through the use of the royal prerogative to by-pass the ordinary courts in their respective spheres of influence, and there is no doubt that in their early days they served a useful purpose. They were suppressed because the Puritans and common-law lawyers of Charles I's day believed they had become instruments of tyranny.[1]

Origins of Legal Dress

King Henry II, a considerate master, provided not only food and wages, but clothes for his servants; and contemporary accounts make it clear that the richness of these clothes was nicely graded according to rank. For example, knights were provided with squirrel fur to adorn their robes while lower orders had to be content with rabbit. Fur, of course, was a highly desirable material to be equipped with to withstand the cold of English winters in the draughty halls of the time; but through its richness and rarity it came to be associated with rank. The earliest documentary evidence we have on legal robes is a royal order of Edward I of the year 1292 ordering the Keeper of the Great Wardrobe to dispense to justices of King's Bench and Common Pleas, and to Barons of the Exchequer, various materials for their robes. These materials, it was ordered, were to be of lighter weight for summer use than for winter, and the same document mentions 'fur of white budge' and 'fur of miniver', together with 'fur of silk'. This injunction points to the origin of the later custom of judges wearing silk edging and lining for summer and autumn terms, and fur for winter and spring terms. The next point to be discovered is the material and colour of these robes.

There can be little doubt that wool was the material used for the robes, this being the stuff of which all contemporary garments of quality were made, except when silk was used for special and rare occasions. English wool was the finest to be obtained in Europe, and it made the finest cloth. The facing and lining of the robes, as we have noted, were of fur or silk according to season.

Until the fourteenth century there does not appear to have been any special colour for judges' robes, but Wardrobe accounts in this century, while bearing this out, establish that green was a favourite. There was as yet no distinction between the robes of chief justices and puisne judges. During the fifteenth century other colours were favoured, but probably the colour, as well as the number and shape of the garments, depended very much on the personal whim of the King. This should not be difficult to understand when it is remembered that legal dress was still largely influenced by the lay fashion of the day. Green still seems to be the favourite, but the records now speak of violet, and violet-pink colours with scarlet hood for winter wear. Royal blue also makes an appearance. By the middle of the century, however, scarlet was rapidly taking the place of other colours, at any rate for chief justices and presiding judges. By the year 1500 scarlet had become the official colour for the Lord High Treasurer presiding over the Court of Exchequer,[2] for the Lords Chief Justice of King's Bench and Common Pleas, and on special occasions for the other judges of King's Bench only. What the Chancellor wore when presiding over the Court of Chancery is, unfortunately, not known. The now familiar Chancellor's robe of black brocade and gold lace did not make its appearance until the late sixteenth century. Until the appointment to this office of Sir Thomas More in 1529 all Chancellors had been churchmen and may well have presided in bishops' convocation robes (for further notes on the Chancellor's robes, see section on page 135).

At the same time that scarlet was becoming the official colour for chief justices, it seems that mustard was being adopted by puisne judges. This is supported by contemporary coloured illustrations of the Courts of Chancery, Exchequer and Common Pleas in session. But by the last quarter of the sixteenth century mustard had been replaced by scarlet for these judges also. No further change was made until 1635, when a famous decree of all the High Court judges in joint session settled the number, style and colour of judicial robes for all occasions. Most of the decisions then reached are in force today (see below).

Articles of Dress worn by Judges from the Fifteenth Century until the Decree of 1635

The Fifteenth Century

The Armelausa: Originally the dress of French nobles and probably derived from the consular robe of late Roman and early Byzantine times, this was the garment that came to be especially associated with medieval judges. In form, it was an ankle-length, loose mantle which was open down the right side only, being fastened with a clasp on the right shoulder. The colour by the end of the century was scarlet for chief justices and judges of the King's Bench; mustard colour for other judges. The Armelausa was lined and trimmed with miniver fur.

The Tabard: A sleeveless garment (see heralds' tabards) reaching below the knee, the tabard was of scarlet cloth and also trimmed with miniver. It would seem that, unlike the armelausa, it was worn at this time only by presiding judges.

The Supertunica: The colour of this robe followed the rule for armelausas. It was worn by all judges and was their basic robe. Trimmed with miniver, it was ankle-length, and by the end of the fifteenth century had acquired a slit down the front which may have been introduced for convenience in putting on. The same slit is to be found on the full-dress robe of a judge today, which in all probability has descended from the medieval supertunica.

The Shoulder-piece and Roller Hood: The former was the lower part of the medieval hood which covered the chest and shoulders. It was scarlet or mustard in colour, trimmed with miniver, and had a short liripipe hanging down the back. It was worn *over* the tabard or supertunica, but *under* the armelausa. Attached to it was the rolled hood of miniver. Considerable modifications in shape and size were to be made to both these garments in the next century.

The Stole, or Tippet: A broad band of silk worn round the neck like a priest's stole. The colour was black, and it hung so that both ends were equidistant below the knees. This likeness to a priest's stole was probably not fortuitous because the first royal judges, like most officials of the Norman and early Plantagenet households, were clerks in holy orders.

The Coif: This was the piece of white linen wound round the head, closely fitted to cover the hair entirely, and then tied under the chin. The coif was always the ornament and symbol of graduation and was never removed, even in the royal presence. It was worn by various high officers of state, as well as by all those to whom the term 'lawyer' can be loosely applied. All these officials belonged to the Order of the Coif, as it was universally known, and the sergeants-at-law from whose ranks the judges were chosen were always members of this order. It is believed that the coif was derived originally from the sweating cap worn by the Knights Templar, and because bestowal of this article of wear formed part of the initiation ceremony of a Knight Templar, it came to be an article specially granted to the King's servants to be

The Coif

worn by them in attendance at court, (cf, royal coif in Chapter 2, on Coronations).

The Skull-cap, or Pileus: All judges wore this cap over the coif. From the evidence afforded by contemporary illustrations it is clear that in style and size the pileus was not like the modern skull-cap perching on the back of the head, but a more close-fitting, round headgear that covered the whole head down as far as ears and forehead. It had a button on top, presumably for ease in lifting. In the fifteenth century the colour varied, sometimes scarlet, sometimes pink or brown.

Some fifteenth-century illuminations show judges wearing turbans over coif and pileus, and these turbans are usually the same colour as the armelausa. The turban was not strictly part of the official robes of a judge, but a lay fashion of the time. We cannot be sure why judges wore them on the bench: it may be because they wished to be in the fashion, or perhaps to keep out the icy blasts of air that must have flowed freely in winter through Westminster and county assize halls.

The Sixteenth Century

During this century there were very few changes in judges' robes. The number of articles of wear remained the same, but there was some modification in size and style. The most important actual change came right at the end of the century, and this was the introduction of an informal attire designed to be worn on ordinary working days. The modification in existing robes was as follows:

The Hood: In the previous century this had been the 'roller hood' attached to the shoulder-piece and ending in a small liripipe. Throughout the sixteenth century the hood became progressively larger, and by the end had become a large miniver bag with a long scarlet liripipe hanging right down the back.

The Coif: The linen coif was no longer tied under the chin, but left with the ends hanging down loose. This change seems to have occurred between 1540 and 1550.

The Pileus Quadratus: This was a four-cornered black velvet cap (sometimes cloth) not stiffened in any way. It was not a modification of the old pileus which, curiously enough, continued to be worn *under* the new pileus. The first appearance of the quadratus cap seems to have been in the reign of Henry VIII about the time of the fall of Wolsey, but it did not come into general use among judges until the beginning of Elizabeth's reign.

The Pileus Quadratus

Informal attire for Judges (late sixteenth century)
Before the end of the century, for all but the most solemn occasions, judges of all divisions of the High Court had taken to wearing a simple robe without the now large and cumbersome hood. Nor, it is presumed, did they wear the armelausa on these working days.

The Casting Hood, or Chaperon: In conformity with the new practice, judges substituted this less cumbersome article for the old hood on working days. It was not really a hood at all, but a scarf or 'chaperon' attached to the gown and hanging down on one side. Originally it had been the scarf attached to the fifteenth-century hat of lay fashion to allow the 'chapeau' to hang down over the shoulder when not actually being worn.

The Gloves: By the end of the century it had become customary for judges to *carry* gloves on all official occasions.

The Collar of 'SS': This was the broad gold collar or chain worn today only by the Lord Chief Justice of England in full state robes. This collar had formerly been worn by a number of royal officers, including the Lord High Steward and the Lord Chancellor, but by an ordinance of 1594 the wearing of the collar was confined to the chief justices of King's Bench and Common Pleas and the Lord Chief Baron.

Robes of the Lord Chief Justice, with Collar of 'SS'

Seventeenth Century until 1635

Such changes in judges' robes as occurred between 1600 and 1635 can be summarised briefly.

The Armelausa: This has become a long miniver mantle falling into a train behind. The opening was now down the middle of the front instead of on the right side.

The Supertunica: This has become a long scarlet robe reaching to the feet. It was distinguished from the medieval supertunica by having the cuffs turned back some inches to display the miniver lining. The slit in front was edged with miniver.

The Coif and Pileus: As in Elizabethan times, the white linen coif has small flaps hanging down at the sides. A black skull-cap lined with scarlet is now worn over the coif, while the pileus quadratus worn over all is now furnished with side pieces.

The Shoulder-piece and Hood: The shoulder-piece remained as in earlier days. The extended hood of late Elizabethan times is now a long miniver-furred affair hanging down the back to below the waist and fastened in front in a V-shape.

The Cincture: An innovation dating from this time is the cincture, or silk band, girding the supertunica robe at the waist. By 1625 this band is being tied in a bow.

This, then, was the robing of High Court judges for solemn occasions such as a royal summons to the Lords and attendance at the courts on great days. Legal bands were not, of course, worn as early as this, but around the neck judges wore the lace or pleated ruff of contemporary lay fashion. It is presumed that the black tippet or stole was also worn.

Undress Robes

It will be remembered that undress robes for working days in court had been introduced at the end of the sixteenth century. The headgear remained the same as for full dress; but the miniver mantle and train (armelausa), scarlet supertunica and full miniver hood were not worn for these less formal occasions. In their place judges were now wearing a black or violet supertunica, shoulder-piece and casting hood. Apparently there was no attempt as yet to allot distinctive colours or style of robe to the various divisions of the High Court. Nor was there a distinction in colour for the seasons of the year; but we may take it that the medieval custom of substituting silk lining and edging for miniver was still followed for summer and autumn law terms.

Seventeenth Century—The Westminster Decree

The general principle laid down by this famous decree of all the royal judges sitting in joint session in the year 1635 was that in future the official dress of His Majesty's judges was to be regulated exactly according to *place* (eg, ceremonies and sittings at Westminster, or at provincial assizes) and *occasion*.

At Westminster

The regulation dress for ordinary days in the law term to be black or violet robe, short mantle and hood underneath mantle, all of the same colour. On Lord Mayor's Day, for church on Sundays, and on certain Holy Days, scarlet robe and casting hood to be worn with black stole (the casting hood on these occasions to be worn on right side, but pinned to left shoulder.) The regulation dress for attendance at the House of Lords or meetings of the Privy Council was to be black or violet robe, stole and scarlet casting hood. On high days scarlet robes to be worn. When wearing scarlet robes, full miniver hood and train (armelausa), etc, the Lords Chief Justice of King's Bench and Common Pleas, and the Lord Chief Baron were to wear their Collars of 'SS'. Finally, a regulation laid it down that for all robes the facing and edging was to be of taffeta in summer from Ascension Day until St Simon and St Jude (28 October), and miniver for the rest of the year.

No mention, it will be noted, was made of the presiding judge of the Chancery Division because this was the Lord Chancellor who, by this date, had his own special robes (see below).

On Circuit of Assize

For the service and sermon at the opening of provincial assizes, and on Sundays at church, all judges were to wear scarlet robe, hood and mantle with stole. In the assize court, the 'criminal' judges were to wear the same dress but without the stole. 'Nisi Prius' judges (civil case judges) were to wear in court scarlet robe, stole and casting hood, The full hood and mantle were, however, to be allowed when the weather was cold. This concession, one imagines, was allowed in the interests of aged judges faced with the ordeal of sitting long hours in ill-heated courtrooms. For in those days trials once begun had to continue without a break until a verdict had been reached.

The most striking difference between the dress regulations for Westminster and for circuit occasions is the insistence on scarlet for working days on circuit. The reason can only be guessed. The Westminster Decree was issued in the reign of Charles I, a monarch who laid special emphasis on the royal prerogative. Perhaps this display of scarlet and miniver in the provinces was part of a deliberate plan to impress the King's provincial subjects with the majesty, not so much of the law, as of the judges who in those days were the King's servants. At Westminster, on the contrary, there were normally plenty of other signs of royal power to be seen.

From the Westminster Decree to Modern Times

Such changes as have taken place in judges' official dress since 1635 have mainly been concerned with their head dress and neck wear. Number, style and colour of robes have undergone comparatively minor modification with the passing centuries.

At the end of this section will be found a summary of the modern regulations on official dress of those new judges called into being by the Judicature Acts of 1872-76 (Lords of Appeal in Ordinary, Master of the Rolls, Lords Justice of Appeal, and President of the Probate, Divorce and Admiralty division.)

The Armelausa (Mantle): By 1635 this medieval mantle had already become much shorter, and by the end of the eighteenth century was to reach not much lower than the waist. Made of scarlet cloth lined with miniver, it was now worn open down the front and secured by a clasp at the neck. Down to the second half of the nineteenth century it was worn on the opening day of assizes and at church on Sunday morning on circuit of assize. It could also still be worn in winter in cold weather.

In modern times the armelausa, now called the Mantle,[3] is worn by judges of the Queen's Bench, Chancery, and Probate Divisions only on the following occasions: attending St Paul's Cathedral in state, the Lord Chancellor's Breakfast, and in court on the first day of Michaelmas law term, and at the House of Lords when the Queen is on the throne.

The Head Dress (the Coif): Between 1635 and 1663, when wigs began to be worn, judges' head dress consisted of white linen coif with the ends hanging loose, black velvet skull-cap, and black four-cornered cap worn over all (pileus quadratus). By the end of this period the coif itself had become much smaller, the side pieces descending only as far as the ears. With the coming of the age of wigs, the coif and skull-cap were reduced to no more than a circular patch of black silk surrounded by a white frill worn on top of the wig. The three-cornered black cap was still worn on occasions.

The Head Dress (the Wig): To the general public, the full-bottomed wig is to an English judge what the crown is to a king, so much so that in the past films and plays with court scenes have shown the judge presiding wearing this kind of wig when he would in real life be wearing a tye wig. It was, of course, not until the wearing of wigs as a lay fashion was introduced into western Europe that judges, in common with everyone else, adopted this form of headgear. All that has happened since is, in effect, that whereas lay persons discarded wigs

The working robe, with bob wig, of one of Her Majesty's judges

after a little more than one hundred and twenty years, judges and other officers of the law have continued to wear them. Introduced into England from the court of Louis XIV, the periwig was in the seventeenth century made in natural hair colours, and thus worn not only by gentlemen of quality but also by the royal judges. It was at this time that the reduced coif and circular skull-cap described above finally disappeared. The black pileus remained, but as periwigs became progressively larger the judges took to carrying these four-cornered caps.

In 1705 came a new lay fashion of wearing white or grey-coloured wigs dressed with pomade or meal, and many, though not all, judges followed this custom. In 1720 began the fashion of wearing tye wigs for all but the most formal occasions. This was a short wig curled at the sides and on the forehead, and with a queue hanging down the back of the neck, tied for neatness with a black ribbon. The tye wig owed its origin to the custom of tying back the cumbersome periwig for convenience when riding. Judges, however, for once did not change with the fashion, but continued to favour the long, full periwig, no doubt because they believed it more befitted the dignity of their office. They were influenced also, one imagines, by the fact that for many years the wearing of the periwig was 'de rigeur' at the courts of George I and George II.

By 1750 the long wig, modified only to the extent of now being flat-crowned and with lappets falling in front of each shoulder, had become recognised exclusively as the head dress of His Majesty's judges. The colour remained white or grey. By 1780 one more change had occurred: although judges continued to wear the full wig for the most formal occasions, they now began to adopt the short tye wig for ordinary working days in court. This tye wig had acquired by 1780 two queues and a vertical curl on top. As we have noted, when wigs went out of fashion for ordinary people—largely because of William Pitt's new tax on hair powder in 1793—judges continued to wear them, probably not because lawyers are conservative in their habits, but because by this time the wig had become in the public mind their special badge or symbol of office. Today, judges of the High Court wear full-bottomed wigs when they wear full scarlet robes, as on the opening day of assizes or for state ceremonies.

It may be of interest to note in passing that bishops of the Church of England also continued to wear wigs long after lay persons had discarded them. The bishops, however, seem mostly to have adopted a different form of short wig, without queue, which had a curl all the way round the base. The well-known painting of Queen Victoria's coronation in 1838 shows Archbishop Howley and other Church dignitaries wearing just such a wig. It is said that Dr Blomfield, Bishop of London, was the last bishop to wear this headgear, which he did until his death in 1855. The wearing of wigs by counsel and other law officers will be discussed in a later section.

Neck Wear: The neck wear of judges and lawyers tended from the first to follow lay fashion, from the narrow white collar turned down over the inner robe or tunic, through Elizabethan and Jacobean ruff, to the elaborate pointed lace collar of Cavalier days. The plain white bands worn by lawyers today made their first appearance in the middle of the seventeenth century. The plainness of this form of neck wear no doubt owed much to Puritan influence, but the newly introduced 'jabot' of lay fashion must have had some influence, and certainly influenced the birth of the lace fall of later days. It might be of interest to record here the story (for which there is no actual proof) that the jabot was invented by Prince Rupert. One day during the Civil War when the Court was at Oxford, the King sent an urgent message commanding the Prince's presence. Rupert dressed in a hurry, and not having time to find and put on a clean lace collar, hastily snatched up a short silk scarf lying to hand and knotted it round his neck. Thus attired he was seen by a number of undergraduates as he crossed Tom Quad on his way to the King's lodgings. The next day half the undergraduates in Oxford were walking round wearing white scarves knotted round their necks!

The fashion thus set continued after the Restoration. During the eighteenth century some judges took to wearing the elaborate lace falls that eighteenth-century elegance decreed for men in the fashion. Today, judges wear plain white bands, and only the Lord Chancellor wears the lace fall on state occasions, although until the second world war the Lord Chief Justice, the Master of the Rolls and certain Law Lords also affected this style.

Under-Dress of Judges: From medieval times this seems to have been the ordinary dress of each period, though no doubt of a quality befitting His Majesty's judges. In Tudor and Stuart times this dress included long hose and doublet with slit shirt, altering with advancing fashion. A direction in the Decree of 1635 orders judges 'when riding on circuit' to wear a sleeved and velvet-faced coat of broadcloth. In the eighteenth century they would naturally take to the longer breeches and hose of the period, and this is essentially what the judges' under dress, at any rate for the most formal occasions, has remained. The regulations published for the Lord Chancellor and Judicial Bench read: 'Court Coat, Waistcoat and Knee Breeches of Black Cloth, Black Silk Stockings, Shoes and Steel Buckles . . . Plain Bands . . . White Gloves and Beaver Hat.' This dress, worn under robes, is appointed to be worn for the Lord Chancellor's Breakfast (opening of Michaelmas law term) and first day's sittings in court; at St Paul's Cathedral, the Lord Mayor's Banquet, and at the House of Lords when the

Queen is on the throne. For attendance at Her Majesty's Court and for other state and semi-state functions, levee dress is prescribed (Black Velvet Coat, etc, with 'Cocked Hat, Stock with Lace ends and Ruffles, Steel Sword and Buckles'). The Law Lords and Lord Chief Justice, being Privy Councillors, would normally wear Privy Councillors' uniform for such occasions. This uniform, described in detail later has today been virtually abandoned, except for coronations and for great officers of state at the opening of Parliament.

House of Lords and Court of Appeal

The House of Lords had won recognition as the supreme court of appeal in the realm in certain instances as far back as the reign of Edward III. Until the passing of the Judicature Acts of 1873-76, the House's judicial functions were exercised by the whole body of peers, spiritual and temporal, sitting as judges of both law and fact under the presidency of the Lord High Steward. The peers wore robes and hats, and the verdict was by majority vote of those peers present. The procedure was for the Lord Steward to call upon each peer, beginning with the youngest baron, to rise in his seat and give his verdict. This he did by placing his left hand on his breast and making his declaration 'on his honour'—peers did not have to swear on oath. (In cases involving the death penalty, the lords spiritual always requested permission to withdraw before the verdict 'saving to their order all rights and privileges to which they were entitled'). By the Acts of 1873-76 these judicial functions of the Lords were restricted to a few 'Lords of Appeal in Ordinary' being 'men of high judicial standing' created not hereditary but life peers only. Originally, only two Law Lords were appointed, but today there are nine and they are always former High Court judges of long standing. Both the Lord Chancellor and the Lord Chief Justice, being peers, may sit with them.

Until 1936, peers of the realm charged with felony could still exercise their 'privilege' of being tried by their fellow peers, that is by the whole body of peers. If Parliament was sitting this was by the House of Lords; if Parliament was in recess it would be the Court of the Lord Steward. In either event it meant judgement by the peers themselves. Following a case in 1935, when a peer charged with manslaughter following a motor accident was acquitted, an Act was passed to abolish trial by peers. Today, the only occasion on which the whole House of Lords might still exercise its old judicial powers would be a trial of impeachment, but this has been in abeyance since the early nineteenth century.

By the same Acts of 1873-76 there was set up a new Court of Appeal whose work was to hear appeals from the trial court of civil actions, and the Master of the Rolls was appointed president of this court, with a limited number of senior judges to assist him as Lord Justices of Appeal.

The Court of Criminal Appeal was set up by legislation in 1907 in answer to the charge that there was no means of appealing against the verdict of a jury in a criminal trial except to the House of Lords on points of law and then only with the Attorney-General's 'fiat'. As the Act calling this new court into being laid down that its membership should be 'no fewer than three judges of the King's (Queen's) Bench sitting together', the regulations on dress are those of the Queen's Bench: 'Scarlet Cloth Robe and Hood, Girdle, Tippet, Scarf, Plain Bands and Tye Wig'.

This court was abolished in 1965, and its responsibilities transferred to the Court of Appeal.

Lords of Appeal in Ordinary

The dress regulations issued by authority are as follows:

When hearing appeals in the House: morning dress.

On other occasions: as Privy Councillors, or Parliamentary robes.

When one thinks of some of the magnificent spectacles that historic trials before the whole House of Lords must have afforded, it seems sad indeed that the outward sign of this most important function of the 'High Court of Parliament' should today be reduced to the sight of a handful of elderly gentlemen sitting in a committee room around a blue-clothed table dressed in black coats and pin-striped trousers. No disrespect is intended to Her Majesty's judges when it is suggested that they do not look the embodiment of the Law's majesty out of their robes. In the case of the Lords of Appeal in Ordinary, although cases are argued in the committee room, judgement is delivered in the Lords' chamber from the Woolsack, and the Lord Chancellor might like to consider the possibility of restoring to these judicial lords the wearing of their Parliamentary robes for this one occasion. If this were done, it would give visible credence to the constitutional theory that the Law Lords do, in fact, give judgement in the name of the whole House of Lords.

The 'other occasions' referred to in the dress regulations presumably include attendance at the House when the Queen is present, when Parliamentary robes will be worn. For levées and state banquets their dress should be Privy Councillor's uniform, but it would seem that this custom has now lapsed.

It should here be noted that the Judicature Acts of the eighteen-seventies did not pass without opposition. After the passing of the first Act into law, one lay peer who had voted against the bill continued his protest by attending judicial sittings, which in those days were still held in the chamber of the House. It is reported that this noble lord actually rose from his bench to deliver his own personal verdict on a case, but that with great dignity the learned Lords of Appeal in Ordinary quietly ignored him and continued delivering their own judgement.

The Court of Appeal: The judges of this court, presided over by the Master of the Rolls, on full state occasions wear not the scarlet and miniver of Queen's Bench and Chancery judges but robes of black damask trimmed with gold lace. The robe is somewhat similar to that worn by the Lord Chancellor, the Speaker of the House of Commons and the Chancellor of the Exchequer. The under-dress is court coat and waistcoat of black cloth, black cloth knee-breeches and silk stockings, and shoes with steel buckles. Full-bottomed wigs are worn with stocks with lace ends or plain bands. Beaver hats are worn or carried.

For ordinary working days in court the Lord Justices of Appeal wear black cloth coat and waistcoat, black silk gown, tye wig and plain bands.

The President of the Probate, Divorce and Admiralty Division wears similar robes for state and working days as do the Lords Justice of Appeal. Puisne judges of Chancery and Probate Divisions wear black silk gowns etc, for working days in court, but the scarlet of judges of Queen's Bench on high days.

The Lord High Chancellor of the Realm

The Lord Chancellor has claims to be considered in more than one chapter of this book for he combines in his person no less than three distinct offices:

(i)   As a great officer of state, in modern times he is 'ex-officio' a member of the Cabinet, and thus holds office for the life of the government only.

(ii) He is head of the judiciary, in which capacity he appoints all new judges and Queen's Counsel, and 'nominates' all new justices of the peace and stipendary magistrates (the Lord Chief Justice, however, is a Prime Minister's appointment); and he is president of the Chancery Division, although in modern times he never sits on actual Chancery cases. He does sometimes preside over the Lords of Appeal in Ordinary, that is, over the House of Lords sitting in its judicial capacity.[4]

(iii) He is chairman of the House of Lords, presiding from the Woolsack over the House's legislative and debating work in the chamber.

Not surprisingly, the Lord Chancellor has different robes for his different functions, but before describing them and discussing their origin, it will be as well to take a look at the Chancellor's office and see how it has evolved to its present position.

The title 'Chancellor' is derived from a Latin word, 'cancella', which means 'a screen'. In the days of Henry I, when the departments of state had not yet separated from the royal household, the Chancellor with his clerks ('clerici') sat behind a *screen* set up in the palace hall for privacy to issue the King's writs and general orders to his subjects throughout the realm. He also had charge of the Great Seal whose impression attached to the parchment writs made them official. Thus from very early days the Chancellor occupied a position of commanding importance in the government, and all political matters had to pass through his hands. In time, he acquired a second title which he still bears: 'Lord Keeper of the King's Conscience'. This was, perhaps, a tribute to the influence he exerted and the confidence reposed in him by his royal master. When the Chancellor and Keeper was a man of outstanding ability he was to all intent 'prime minister', though, of course, until kings ceased to exercise full executive power there could be no prime minister in the modern sense.

Throughout the middle ages the Chancellor was almost always a bishop or archbishop. This was because the office required both scholarly and administrative talents, qualities in medieval times found usually only in the ranks of churchmen.[5] Thus it came about that, under the King, England came to be ruled by such able churchmen as Archbishops Becket, Hubert Walter and Thomas Wolsey, and Bishop Stephen Gardiner. The last ecclesiastical Lord Chancellor was Dr Nicholas Heath, Archbishop of York, who resigned the office some two months after Elizabeth I ascended the throne in November 1558.

Thereafter no more churchmen were appointed to this office. The Reformation had, of course, created a bias against ecclesiastical domination, and the 'New Learning' had created a professional class of lawyers well qualified to fill this high office.

We have noted elsewhere that the first lay Chancellor, Sir Thomas More, was never raised to the peerage and so, although he presided over sessions of the Lords, he had no vote. Sir Thomas Audley, More's successor, was created a peer specially to fit him for that office. Some years later Queen Elizabeth made Sir Nicholas Bacon Lord Keeper, but denied him the title of Chancellor. Nor was he ever given a peerage. Bacon's successor, Sir Christopher Hatton, was also denied a peerage, although he was given the superior title of Chancellor. What one deduces from this is that, by late Tudor times, although a knowledge and professional experience of the law was considered an essential qualification for the Chancellorship, a peerage was not. As both Tudor and Stuart monarchs treated their Chancellors and Lord Keepers as their 'mouthpiece' for declaring to their parliaments the royal will and policy, a peerage no doubt seemed of secondary importance. The last Lord Chancellor to act as chief minister was Edward Hyde, Earl of Clarendon, Lord Chancellor for the first seven years after the Restoration. Thereafter, with the doubtful exceptions of Anthony Ashley Cooper, first Earl of Shaftesbury, and Lord Chancellor Jeffreys of Bloody Assize notoriety, the Lord Chancellors were limited to their judicial and parliamentary functions.

Robes of the Lord Chancellor

When we come to consider the history of the Lord Chancellor's robes we are struck by the fact that, until the end of the sixteenth century, there does not seem to have been any distinctive livery or robe which went with the office. Thomas Becket, though technically in minor orders when he was Chancellor, probably wore a particularly rich form of the supertunica and knightly hauberk, since we know he was addicted to lay attire until he became Archbishop of Canterbury. There were, of course, no peers' robes in those days. Throughout the middle ages the Chancellors being bishops, and therefore what the next age would call lords spiritual, very likely wore in the Lords, that is in Parliament, the habit and chasuble or cope and mitre of their religious order. When we come to Wolsey's long reign as Chancellor (1515-29) we have evidence that that magnificent prelate clothed himself in the scarlet of his cardinalate. We know also that he seldom went anywhere without an accompanying procession consisting of eight silver-mace bearers dressed in red liveries, a priest carrying the Red Hat, and a gentleman richly attired carrying the Great Seal in its Purse, all preceding the Chancellor, who was followed by a veritable concourse of gentlemen, chaplains, grooms of the chamber and so forth. The Cardinal was always a master of pageantry and had a fine sense of theatre. By way of dramatic contrast, the next Chancellor, More, seems to have been content to wear a simple long gown, though this was fur trimmed, and he wore, too, his gold Collar of 'SS'. More was not a peer; those of his lay successors who were would almost certainly have worn the peer's parliamentary robe of their degree.

The black damask robe or gown embroidered with gold lace, and having winged sleeves and gold tassels, which the Chancellor today wears on state occasions, originated as a form of lay fashion for dignitaries in the late sixteenth century. Sir Thomas Egerton, Queen Elizabeth's Lord Keeper for the last years of her reign, who later became King James's first Lord Chancellor, with the titles of Lord Ellesmere and Viscount Brackley, may have been the first Chancellor officially to have worn this robe. Certainly his successor, Francis Bacon, Viscount St Albans, wore it, as a famous portrait clearly shows. We may say, therefore, that from the beginning of the seventeenth century this black and gold brocade gown became the Chancellor's official robe and, except for a lengthening at the back in the form of a short train, it has remained practically unaltered up to the present day.

As a footnote to this section, it is interesting that, in about the year 1617, the same type of robe became the official dress of the chancellors of the universities of Oxford and Cambridge, the only marked difference being the addition to the university chancellors' robes of gold rosettes on the sleeves and in the centre of the train. In the same century this form of robe seems to have been worn on certain occasions by Privy Councillors, and this no doubt accounts for the fact that it is also the official robe of the Chancellor of the Exchequer, although today a coronation is about the only occasion on which that minister wears it.

The Lord Chancellor's Head Dress

Until the beginning of the eighteenth century, the head dress proper to the office was simply a lay hat of the period. Francis Bacon is shown in a contemporary portrait in Chancellor's robes wearing also the tall steeple hat of the early Jacobean period. By the eighteenth century this hat had become the tricorn, and so it has remained. The wig was

Robes of the Lord Chancellor and Purse containing the Great Seal

adopted at the same time as the judges', and like them has been retained by Chancellors after lay persons had abandoned it. Unlike judges, however, the Lord Chancellor has never appeared in a tye wig. Today, to all intents and purposes, the full-bottomed wig *is* the head dress of the Lord Chancellor, the occasions on which he wears the tricorn being rare, such as at the ceremony of introducing a new peer to Parliament or when presiding over a sitting of a Royal Commission in the Lords.

When the House of Lords goes into committee of the whole House the Lord Chancellor leaves the Woolsack and removes his wig and black gown to take his seat on the Treasury bench. He is, of course, wearing his black cloth coat and knee-breeches, and he does not again don wig and gown until the House resumes and he returns to his seat on the Woolsack. While presiding from the Woolsack, the Chancellor may in general debate make a political speech or answer questions on behalf of the government, of which he is a member. On such occasions he rises from the Woolsack and takes three paces to the right before speaking. By this old convention is symbolically preserved the constitutional principle of the separation of his powers—as an executive minister of the Crown, and as the impartial chairman of the legislative assembly.

The House of Lord's mace and the Chancellor's purse are carried before him on entry into the chamber and placed at the back of the Woolsack, there to remain so long as the House is in session. Mace and purse are also carried before him on all state occasions when he goes in procession. In theory, the purse carries the Great Seal of the Realm. In practice, it has not done so for a very long time. (Legend has it that an eighteenth-century Chancellor dropped the purse which then did contain the Great Seal, and such was its weight that it broke a bone in his foot.)

Sergeants-at-Law

The office and rank of sergeant-at-law is very ancient, at least as old as that of judge. From the time of Edward I until their influence began to decline in the eighteenth century, the sergeants were to the legal profession what Queen's Counsel are today, and like them their principal work lay in pleading in the courts. Devotees of the *Pickwick Papers* will not need to be reminded of the colourful personality of Mr Pickwick's formidable court adversary, Sergeant Buzfuz. The Order of Sergeants was abolished in England in 1877, but a few existing sergeants continued to practice alongside the barristers who had superseded them until death or retirement removed the last trace of this once famous order. The last sergeant-at-law to practice in the English courts was not an English sergeant at all, having received his sergeant's call at the Irish Bar. This was Sergeant Sullivan who, in the first quarter of this century, made a considerable reputation at the English Bar as a King's Counsel. Among many famous cases, he figured as leading counsel for the defence in Roger Casement's trial for treason, and continued to practice until well into the nineteen-thirties.

Official Dress of Sergeants

Sergeants were members of the Order of the Coif, and the royal judges were habitually chosen from the ranks of the senior sergeants of this order. As we can expect, the wearing of the coif formed an important part of a sergeant's investiture.

By the middle of the fourteenth century the sergeant's robes consisted of a sleeveless tabard *or* a full-length supertunica with narrow sleeves. Sergeants were not allowed the armelausa, but they were given shoulder-pieces and hoods. It was further laid down that the linings and edgings of their robes must be of lamb's wool only (miniver was reserved for judges). The robe was girded at the waist, and the flat hood which was attached to a roll of fur round the neck fell half-way down the back. The colour of the robes in this early period seems to have varied, but blue was probably a favourite.

The next important development in sergeants' dress was the parti-coloured robe. Like so much else in official dress, this originated in a contemporary lay fashion. At the court of Richard II, not only had short tunic and long hose become fashionable, but the further refinement of a vertical division of colour had been adopted. Thus the well-dressed gentleman appeared in doublet and hose, red or blue on one side from neck to toe, green or yellow on the other. The traditional livery of the court jester was only aping the normal costume of his betters. Sergeants-at-law, therefore, were merely extending this sartorial principle to embrace their long robes which, in the following century, were usually blue and green, sometimes with thin white stripes added; hood and cape were also worn parti-coloured.

In the first half of the sixteenth century other colours made their appearance, in particular brown-blue, mustard-murrey, and violet in grain. At the same time the sergeants acquired the right to wear scarlet, starting with the hood. We learn that at a ceremony of creation of sergeants in Henry VIII's reign the new sergeants wore blue supertunicas in procession to Westminster Hall, each with his servant carrying before him the linen coif and scarlet hood. These emblems of rank were then ceremonially handed to each sergeant by the seated judges, and worn at the feast which always followed the ceremony.

Robe and wig of a Sergeant-at-Law

Although parti-coloured robes were insisted on for ceremonies of creation during the rest of this century, the tendency was for a robe of one colour—usually violet—to be worn on all other official occasions except the grandest when they were permitted to wear scarlet robes.

In the next century we find that the Westminster Decree also issued regulations on the dress of sergeants. On Sundays and special days they were ordered to wear scarlet robe, shoulder-piece, small hood and large liripipe also in scarlet, like the judges, but different from the latter in having the hood closed. On other days the sergeants were to wear parti-coloured black and murrey for their first year, and thereafter an open gown of purple cloth with scarlet hood over the right shoulder for bar or circuit work.

By the year 1700 a black lace gown with square-cut lace collar had been adopted. The last general call of sergeants ever to be held was at Westminster Hall in 1736, and for their presentation at this ceremony the new sergeants wore black lace (barristers') gowns and full-bottomed wigs. They then received from the judges their scarlet hoods and coifs; but immediately after they put on purple and murrey parti-coloured robes and carried in their hands black square caps (the pileus quadratus?) There is one further record from the year 1762, when we are told that a new sergeant wore parti-coloured robes for his presentation and the feast that followed, after which he changed into a black silk gown. This seems to have been the last occasion on which a parti-coloured gown was worn. Thereafter the history of the sergeants' robing until their suppression in 1877 was one of modification to the black lace gown out of which developed the silk gown of the King's Counsel.

Barristers-at-Law

One result of the great law reforms of Edward I at the end of the thirteenth century was a remarkable increase in the number of cases the sergeants had to cope with in the courts. It is from this reign that they acquired the right to call in apprentices to assist them. These 'apprentices-at-law' were ordered to attend court and learn the law by their attendance. Later they were given the name 'barrister', probably because they attended 'at the Bar' (the exact derivation of the word is unknown), and acquired the right to plead on their own. At the same time they also began to undermine the position long held by the sergeants, so that in the end they came to supersede them. The rise in importance of the barristers may be attributed to the clause in Magna Carta which fixed the Court of Common Pleas at Westminster, with the consequence that the 'professors of law' were brought together in London. We learn that associations of lawyers from this time acquired houses of their own in which students were educated in the common law for the degree of barrister (apprentice or bachelor) and of sergeant (doctor). These schools of lawyers are now represented by the Inns of Court which still enjoy the exclusive privilege of conducting law examinations and calling to the Bar. With the passing of the Judicature Acts of 1873-76, pleading in the High Court became the exclusive prerogative of the order of barristers called by the Inns of Court.

King's (Queen's) Counsel

These are really senior barristers of so many years standing and experience who, on application to the Lord Chancellor of the day, have been called by him 'within the Bar'. Their work is largely concerned with pleading in the more important cases. They are not a separate order of lawyers. In modern times, the chief law officers of the Crown, the Attorney-General and the Solicitor-General, are always Queen's Counsel (QCs).

The origin of these eminent members of the legal profession seems to have been somewhat disreputable. We first hear of them in the sixteenth century acting as assistants to the Attorney- and Solicitor-General. By the year 1604 their position was firmly established; but on somewhat dubious foundations. It would appear that King James, who had need to bend the law to suit his own interpretation of the powers allowed through the royal prerogative, decided to collect round him a select band of counsel well skilled in the law who might be bribed to use their skill in the courts on the King's behalf. The inference is that the sergeants were either too honest or, being of the Puritan persuasion, too opposed on religio-political grounds to serve the royal purpose. The King's Counsel continued, small in numbers, as court favourites until well into the eighteenth century, and most of these gentlemen seem to have secured their title (and no doubt more material advantages) by bribery or flattery. It was not until the reign of William IV that they emerged to take up the position of eminence and integrity they have enjoyed ever since.

Dress of Barristers

In early days the apprentices (barristers) seem to have worn the supertunica of sergeants, but of one colour, usually blue. They did not acquire either the parti-coloured robe or the scarlet granted to the sergeants. By the seventeenth century they had come to adopt the black lace gown favoured by the sergeants for court work, and this gown was the forerunner of the barrister's gown of today. Not being members of the Order of the Coif, they never acquired the right to wear this head dress, but they continued to wear the wig in company with judges and sergeants after lay persons had discarded it. Today

Queen's Counsel, as the successors in authority of the old sergeants, wear black silk gowns, while other barristers wear 'stuff' (cloth) gowns. The QCs also, on state occasions, such as the Lord Chancellor's Breakfast and attendance at the House of Lords, wear full-bottomed wigs and an under-dress of court coat, breeches and silk stockings with buckled shoes.

Attorneys and Solicitors

The attorneys were 'outside the Bar', and therefore lawyers of inferior rank. They had their headquarters at the Inns of Chancery, and were largely employed in common-law work. They do not appear to have acquired any special robes of rank.

The solicitors, as distinct from attorneys, did not make their appearance until the fifteenth century. They also were employed in Chancery work. In the eighteenth century this work was taken over by the attorneys, and in their old capacity they ceased to exist. The development of the work of solicitors in modern times dates from the nineteenth century, and it is from this period that solicitors acquired a black stuff gown of rank, the chief feature of which is a shallower collar and less embroidery. Solicitors, being in their modern form a late creation, have no historic reason to wear wigs.

5 KNIGHTHOOD: INSIGNIA AND ROBES OF ORDERS OF CHIVALRY

1 : History of Knighthood

Of the many surviving occasions of ancient ceremonial display not the least splendid are the annual chapters of certain orders of chivalry when Her Majesty the Queen is present as Sovereign Head of these orders. Before relating their history and describing robes and insignia of these orders, it will be useful to describe briefly the origins of knighthood, and follow the development of this 'rank, style and privilege' into the three divisions of Knights Bachelor, Baronets, and Membership of Orders of Chivalry.

The word 'knight' is derived from the Anglo-Saxon *cniht*. The exact meaning is uncertain: in Saxon times it seems to have meant 'boy' or 'youth', and an obligation to undertake military service for a certain number of days on behalf of the thegn, or lord. Before the middle of the twelfth century the word had acquired the same meaning as that attached to the French *chevalier*, though this had as yet little to do with that elaborate code of knightly conduct which the Catholic Church and Christian monarchs in western Europe impressed on this warrior class in the later middle ages. The knight of the twelfth and thirteenth century was an altogether sterner figure, a trained fighting man who, in return for the tenure of land, for which he did homage, undertook to fight with horse, lance, sword and shield for his feudal lord. Savage and cruel as he must often have been, it was his fighting quality and discipline that saved Europe from lapsing back into barbarism.

It was the fourteenth century that gave birth to the 'Age of Chivalry' and the knight of romance. The Catholic Church, everywhere seeking to curb the bestiality of medieval warfare, encouraged the adoption of a new code of manners and chivalric conduct by these fierce warrior knights. In England, this new spirit owed much to the genius of a young warrior king. Of Edward III (1327-77) Sir Arthur Bryant has written:

'Splendid in armour and emblazonry, Edward seemed to the young English nobles the very reincarnation of their hero, King Arthur. It was so that he saw himself—the crowned leader of a brotherhood of Christian knights'.

This new ideal of chivalry marked an immense advance on the old code which Sir Arthur Bryant has described as 'the old suicidal law of tribal vengeance and the bloody anarchy of might'. And so there grew up in western Europe during this century, as the outward and visible form of this new conception of knighthood, an elaborate system of training, initiation and rules of conduct, coupled with a widespread enthusiasm for heraldic pageantry, costly armour and meticulous regard for details of ceremony. And all this found expression not only in the tournament, but on the actual field of battle. It is impossible to read Sir John Froissart's account of Crecy and Poitiers without being conscious of the fact that, in spite of the blood and cruelty, there was much of the spirit of the tournament with its true chivalry in the conduct of those famous battles. The adaptation of gunpowder to warfare, and the rise of the national state with its political doctrine of realism, eventually killed the ideal of chivalry, though the outward forms persisted in the tournament for another century. From the sixteenth century onwards, however, the bestowal of knighthood came increasingly to be regarded as a political honour, and so it remains today. Only in one or two of the older orders of chivalry are still to be found traces of the once universal ideal of a Christian code of knighthood. Perhaps this is what Lord Melbourne was reaching for when he said he liked 'the Garter' because there was 'no damn merit about it'.

The Order of Knights Bachelor

This is the oldest existing form of knighthood, predating the earliest of the orders of chivalry by some centuries. It has been said that there were two kinds of knights bachelor, but the distinction seems to have arisen only because there were in those days two alternative ceremonies by which the honour might be conferred.

Knights of the Sword: This was the appellation unofficially bestowed on those knights who received their initiation and 'accolade' on the field of battle as an immediate reward for an outstanding feat of valour and leadership. The word 'accolade' itself is derived from two Latin words: *ad* = 'to', and *collum* = 'neck'. To receive the accolade meant to receive a blow or tap on the shoulder with the sword. This ceremony usually included also an embrace by the king or nobleman bestowing the knighthood and a slight smack on the cheek, the latter probably having originated in the Roman custom of a master striking his slave for the last time at the ceremony granting him his freedom. In the nature of things the new knight was not subjected to an elaborate ceremony entailing the putting on of ceremonial garments; but no doubt at the first opportunity he would don knightly 'coat of arms' blazoned with the device he had chosen or had had allotted to him by the heralds, and he would acquire the new armour and golden spurs of his rank.

Knights of the Bath: This was the name that came to be bestowed on those who received their accolade in palace or castle chapel after a long period of training and preparation, first as pages then as esquires. The title was adopted because the taking of a ceremonial bath formed part of the initiation ceremony of candidates for knighthood. It is important to understand that the order of chivalry known as 'The Most Honourable Order of the Bath' was as yet unborn, was not in fact to come into existence until the eighteenth century. Yet this eighteenth-century order which we shall presently be looking at did have its prototype in the special circumstances attending the creation of a number of knights in 1399 by the Lancastrian King Henry IV to assist at his coronation. These special circumstances will be noted in the section dealing with the Order of the Bath. We must now describe the long process by which the well-born youth graduated to knighthood.

The process began when the future knight, as a boy of nine or ten, was placed in a noble household as a *page*. In that capacity he was taught to serve at table, to read and write French, the universal language of chivalry, and a great deal of the ordinary administrative duties of running a large feudal household. He was constantly in attendance on his master and his mistress, and learnt the graces of discipline and courtesy. Even as a boy he was given instruction in military arts, and learnt to cast a spear, sustain a shield, ride correctly and march on foot with measured tread. He was also inducted into the mysteries of the hunt, both with hounds and falconry. When he reached the age of fifteen or sixteen the page became an *esquire*, a word derived from the French *escurier*, meaning 'a shield-bearer'. As an esquire, he became responsible for carrying his master's shield, and following him into battle. His duties included arming his master before a battle or tournament, and fighting by his side. Once a page was appointed esquire to lord or knight he was considered to have attained to the rank of gentleman with the right to bear his own arms. He was given a sword, but not a knight's belt; and although he now wore full armour himself, this differed in several respects from that of a knight. There does not appear to have been any special ceremony of investiture for esquires unless they were in the personal service of the King. In which case they were presented with silver spurs and a silver collar. After a period of six or seven years, during which he had borne himself worthily and bravely, and proved his skill in weapons, the esquire was considered ready for knighthood. Not all esquires, be it noted, either expected or wished to qualify for the accolade: there are many instances of men being content to serve as esquires all their lives, and not a few attained fame and glory in this comparatively lowly position. At Barnet, in 1471, John Milwater and Thomas à Parr, both esquires of Richard, Duke of Gloucester, fell in battle defending their master to the end. For those who were called to knighthood the ceremonies of initiation were as follows:

The process of knight-making began some two days before the conferring of the final accolade when the candidate, having divested himself of his esquire's livery, took a bath—an event sufficiently unusual in the middle ages to mark a special occasion. In this case the bath was symbolic of purification. On rising from his bath the candidate was solemnly robed in a number of garments, each one having attached to it some symbolic meaning: first, a white tunic symbolic of purity; over this was placed a red robe signifying the blood he must as a knight be prepared to shed in defence of the Faith; there followed a black doublet emblematic of the death that awaited him and all mankind; while, finally, there was girded round him a white belt as a sign of chastity. Thus vested he was required to fast for twenty-four hours. Then, having broken his fast, he went to the chapel where, with his new sword laid up on the altar, he kept a night-long vigil on his knees in prayer. In the early morning, after making his confession, he heard Mass and received the Sacrament in the presence of the nobleman from whom he was to receive the accolade, and his attendant knights and esquires. The new sword was blessed by the priest, and finally the candidate knelt before the nobleman and took the oath to be a true knight and to bear himself bravely and honourably in all his dealings.

The Black Prince

Two knight sponsors then invested him: the golden spurs were fastened to his heels, his new armour was placed on him piece by piece, ending with gauntlets and helmet, and the blessed sword was girded on. Then, kneeling once more, he was tapped three times with the sword on the shoulder in honour of the Holy Trinity, and was given a slight slap on the cheek. Just before the accolade the nobleman said: '*Soyez bon chevalier au nom de Dieu et Saint George*'. Then, after the cheek blow he said: '*Avencez*', and the new knight rose from his knees to be led in procession from the chapel to the castle bailey where his destrier, fully caparisoned, was waiting. Still attired in his knight's armour and with lance erect, he then rode off amid acclamation to show himself to the large crowd of people that always assembled for these occasions. Later that day there would be feasting and dancing in the hall of the castle.

Knights Banneret: These knights were not a separate order, but knights bachelor of the middle ages who, by virtue of feudal status or skill and bravery in warfare, had commended themselves specially to the prince with whom they served. Unlike ordinary knights bachelor, the banneret's knighthood was not based on feudal tenure, but on personal service to the prince or king. A distinguishing mark, one that perhaps may have earned them their name, was that unlike ordinary knights who were granted pennons only, they were accorded the right to fly banners, a privilege previously granted only to earls and barons. Froissart has described how that famous paladin, Sir John Chandos, himself a founder Knight of the Garter, was made a banneret by the Black Prince in 1367 on the morning of the battle of Najera in Spain. It is worth quoting in modern English his actual description of the scene:

> The troops being drawn up in battle order before the action commenced, Sir John advanced in front of the battalions with his banner uncased in his hand. He presented it to the Prince, saying:
>
> 'My lord, here is my banner; I present it to you that I may display it in whatever manner shall be most agreeable to you; for, thanks to God, I have now sufficient lands to enable me to do so and maintain the rank which it ought to hold.'
>
> The Prince, Don Pedro being present, took the banner in his hands, which was blazoned with a sharp stake gules on a field argent; after having cut off the tail to make it square, he displayed it, and returning it to him by the handle said:
>
> 'Sir John, I return to you your banner; God give you strength and honour to preserve it'.
>
> Upon this Sir John left the Prince, went back to his men with the banner in his hand, and said to them:
>
> 'Gentlemen, behold my banner and yours; you will therefore guard it as it becomes you'.
>
> His companions, taking the banner, replied with much cheerfulness that if it pleased God and St George they would defend it well and act worthily of it to the utmost of their abilities.

The Prince was Pedro the Cruel, the deposed King of Aragon, whom the Black Prince and the English were fighting to restore to the throne usurped by Henry of Trastemara, who was supported by the French.

Although the knights bachelor are the eldest of all the English orders of knights, they are not a royal order. It was not until 1926 that George V gave royal approval for a badge. This is an oval of vermilion-painted enamel bearing as a device an upright sword between two spurs, surrounded by a sword belt, and all gilt. The badge, which measures 3in by 2in, is not worn with a ribbon round the neck as with other orders, but as a star on the breast.

The Order of Baronets

This is the only hereditary order of knighthood. It was created by James I and VI in 1611. The idea behind the foundation was that the King, who at that time had need for some ready cash, might obtain from the sale of this new honour which conferred rank, precedence and title but no special privilege, the sum of £1,095 for every baronetcy. This was the amount estimated necessary to maintain thirty infantrymen for three years in Ulster, where James had set up his new Protestant settlement. It is believed that the title 'Baronet' commended itself to the King because the new order was to be hereditary, like the rank of baron, but without the privilege of peerage. Another theory is that the word is a synonym of 'banneret'. The first knight baronet to be created was Sir Nicholas Bacon, Queen Elizabeth's old Lord Keeper and father of Francis Bacon.

The Badge of the Order: Charles I instituted the wearing of a badge by knights baronet, but this badge does not seem to have out-lasted his reign. It was not until 1929 that George V granted the order the privilege of wearing an official badge, on an orange ribbon with dark blue edges, round the neck.

The badge consisted of a reproduction of the arms granted by King James: the arms of Ulster (a red left hand) on a shield argent surmounted by an imperial crown proper within an oval pierced wreath of roses, thistles and shamrocks. This shield to be borne as a canton or inescutcheon in the arms of the owner. The 'bloody hand of Ulster' has been borne ever since on the arms of all baronets.

2 : The Orders of Chivalry

There are nine British orders of chivalry conferring rank, title and precedence over which the Queen presides as Sovereign Head. In order of seniority with the date of foundation these are:

The Most Noble Order of the Garter (1348)
The Most Ancient and Most Noble Order of the Thistle (1702)
The Most Honourable Order of the Bath (1725)
The Most Illustrious Order of St Patrick (1783)
The Most Distinguished Order of St Michael and St George (1818)
The Most Exalted Order of the Star of India (1861)
The Most Eminent Order of the Indian Empire (1877)
The Royal Victorian Order (1896)
The Most Excellent Order of the British Empire (1917)

Since the creation of the Irish Free State (now the Republic of Eire) in 1922, no new creations of Knights of St Patrick have been made, nor have any chapters of the order been held. The last appointment to this order was that of the Duke of Abercorn, first Governor-General of Northern Ireland. The only surviving Knight Companion (1970) is HRH the Duke of Gloucester.

A similar situation prevails as regards the two Indian orders, to which no appointments have been made since Independence in 1947.

The remaining six orders are all flourishing, and descriptions of their separate histories and illustrations of their insignia follow. At the end of the chapter there is also a short history and description of a tenth order, the Venerable Order of the Hospital of St John of Jerusalem. For reasons which are explained, this order does not find a place among the royal orders of knighthood listed above; but because of its interesting history and antecedents, as well as its present control of that well-known institution, the St John Ambulance Brigade, it has been thought proper to include it.

The Most Noble Order of the Garter

Motto: '*Honi Soit Qui Mal Y Pense*' ('Let Shame be to Him who Thinks Evil').

This is the oldest surviving order of chivalry in Europe, and it predates the foundation of that great European order, the Burgundian-Hapsburg 'Toisson D'Or' (the Golden Fleece) by ninety years. Founded by Edward III in honour of the Holy Trinity, the Blessed Virgin Mary, St George and St Edward the Confessor (the last two respectively principal patron of England and patron of English kings), the exact date of foundation is uncertain, but it is believed to have been the year 1348 in the following circumstances:

To commemorate the resounding English victory over the French in the Hundred Years War at Crecy (1346), King Edward on his return to England determined to give practical effect to an idea he had been considering for some time, that is to establish in his realm a new order of chivalry which should be based on the legend of King Arthur and his knights of the Round Table. Although Sir Thomas Mallory was not to produce his *Morte D'Arthur* for one hundred years, by the middle of the fourteenth century it had become the fashion for the English knight to model his life on a romantic conception of the Arthurian knight, and it had seemed altogether appropriate to the English king to 'revive' in some form the Order of the Round Table.

The victory of Crecy made Edward even more determined to go ahead with his foundation; but now he decided for some reason to alter the original dedication. One obvious reason is that, in Catholic medieval Europe, dedication to God and the saints was a *sine qua non* of respectability. In any case, ever since the early Crusades St George had been considered to have England specially under his protection. He was now to become not only the patron of the Garter, but the patron of England. The King decided that the order should consist of himself as Sovereign Head and twenty-five Knights Companion of St George linked together by vows of friendship and dedicated to the 'advancement of piety, nobility and chivalry'. The original chapel at Windsor Castle dedicated to St Edward the Confessor was to become the chapel of the order, and on 6 August 1348 orders were issued for its conversion into one of 'befitting splendour' to serve the new knighthood.

At the same time provision was made for the number of canons of Windsor to be increased from eight to twelve.[1] There were also to be thirteen priests or 'vicars' attached to the chapel, who together with the canons, would make the total number of clergy equal to that of the Knights Companion. Also appointed was a dean to preside over the clergy, and the Bishop of Winchester, within whose diocese Windsor then lay, was appointed Prelate of the Order.[2] Finally, the King made provision for twenty-four old soldiers of gentle birth ('helpless and indifferent knights') to be known as 'the Poor Knights of Windsor'. Their duty was to be present at all future chapters of the order to attend on the Knights Companion. In return they were to receive food and lodging for the rest of their lives, the cost to be provided out of the order's funds. Five hundred years later King William IV changed

The Star of the Order of the Garter

The Collar of the Order of the Garter

their name to the 'Military Knights of Windsor'. They are still recruited from the ranks of retired regular Army officers, usually of high rank; and a certain number are always on duty at Windsor Castle, attending services in St George's Chapel and, of course, all Garter ceremonies. These Military Knights live in a charming little row of cottages lining the approach to the Round Tower, receiving 'board and lodging' as did King Edward's 'Poor Knights'.

As we have noted, at first Edward III seems to have intended his new order to be named the Companionship of St George. But according to the legend, at a ball held at Calais after its capture in 1347, the loveliest woman in England, Joan the Fair Maid of Kent, wife of the Earl of Salisbury and later of the Black Prince himself, dropped her garter accidentally while dancing. The King himself retrieved it. The courtiers observing the incident sniggered, whereupon the King put the garter on his own leg remarking sternly: '*Honi soit qui mal y pense*'! (French was still the official language of the Court). Whether or not this charming story is based on historical fact, we do know for certain that after his return from Calais the King ordered for himself and the first knights of his order twelve garters of royal blue embroidered in gold with those words attributed to him, and the cross of St George.

The new knights wore this insignia for the first time at a tournament held at Eltham in January 1348 (Bryant: *Age of Chivalry*). That there were to be no half measures in setting up the new order in splendour is evidenced by the placing of an order that same year for 'standards with a leopard entire at the head and underneath the arms of St George' together with 'eight hundred pennovells (pennants) of the arms of St George for the lances of the King's esquires and other men-at-arms'. (Bryant: *Age of Chivalry*). On St George's Day, 23 April 1349, while England was still in the grip of the terrible Black Death, the first service of the Order of the Garter was held at Windsor. This time the Knights Companion wore not only their garter insignia[3], but mantles, hoods, and tunics all blue (in honour of the Blessed Virgin?) and plumes to their hats. Hoods and mantles were lined with miniver fur, the sovereign's with ermine.

This, then, was the original dress of the Knights of the Garter, and there have been only one or two items of insignia added since in all the order's long history. The gold collar or chain with its pendent badge called 'the George' was added by Henry VII. The last innovation was made by Charles II to whose command is owed the custom of wearing a broad blue riband over the left shoulder with the jewelled badge known as 'the Lesser George' clasping the ends of the riband on the right hip. This riband, which is never worn with the collar or full robes, took the place of a narrow blue ribbon hung round the neck and from which was suspended the Lesser George in earlier days, as may be noted from Vandyck's famous portrait of Charles I. The colour of the riband has been altered on several occasions. In Stuart times it was of a much lighter shade of blue than it afterwards became. It is said that the Hanoverian monarchs altered it to kingfisher blue to distinguish their order from that of the exiled Stuart monarchs, who continued to bestow the coveted decoration on their Jacobite supporters. In 1950, George VI changed the shade of blue once again.

Ladies have been admitted to the Order of the Garter since its foundation—Froissart has described the appearance of Queen Philippa at the first feast ever held. But appointments seem to have been few and confined to ladies of royal blood, with one or two notable exceptions such as Alice Chaucer, grand-daughter of the poet and herself wife of William de la Pole, first Duke of Suffolk. These ladies received the title, 'Dame de la Fraternité de Saint George'. The appointment of lady members fell into abeyance at the end of the middle ages, the last appointments being those of the Princesses Margaret and Mary Tudor, daughters of Henry VII. An attempt was made by Charles I to revive such appointments, but the pressure of political events in his reign doomed it to failure. Under Charles II, according to Elias Ashmole, the great historian of the order (see Chapter 1, on Heraldry), it was agreed in chapter that ladies should be readmitted, and Queen Katherine of Braganza signified her willingness to become the first Lady of the Garter under the new dispensation. But for some reason or other the matter was never followed up, and it was left for Queen Anne to effect such a restoration, which she did by attending chapters in the capacity of Sovereign of the Order in 1702 and again in 1704. We are told that the Queen wore the Garter itself round her left arm, and this custom has been followed ever since. Today, apart from Her present Majesty as Sovereign, there are only two living Ladies of the Garter, Her Majesty the Queen Mother and Her Majesty the Queen of the Netherlands. (See colour illustration, p. 87.)

The original constitution of the order was first amended by George III who ordained that in future royal princes, being direct descendants of George II, might be admitted Knights even if the original number of twenty-five be exceeded. No doubt the purpose of this conscientious, well-meaning monarch was to accommodate his prolific family, and certainly we have grown accustomed to the sight of the famous Star and Riband gracing the coats of most of the male members of King George's family down to Victoria's day, as the many royal portraits testify.

One curious inconsistency in respect of qualification for membership presents itself: in what may be called the definitive biography of Rufus Isaacs, first Marquess of Reading, H. Montgomery Hyde states that, on his retirement from the office of Viceroy of India in 1926, Lord Reading, then an earl, was advanced in the peerage to the dignity of a marquisate instead of being offered the Garter as was customary because 'the premier order of chivalry in the world has always been confined to Christians' (Lord Reading was, of course, a Jew). Yet Queen Victoria had twice conferred this great Christian order on non-Christians when Lord Reading was a small boy—on the Sultan of Turkey in 1867, and on the Shah of Persia in 1873. Presumably, the rule did not apply to the appointment of heads of state in an honorary capacity.

The disposal of membership of this great order has, of course, like that of all the other royal orders, always lain with the royal prerogative; but since the beginning of the eighteenth century and the rise of constitutional monarchy the sovereign has always consulted the prime minister of the day before making any appointment. The Garter thus became, in effect, a political award and remained so for nearly two hundred and fifty years. On 4 December 1946, to mark the seven hundredth anniversary of the order's foundation, the Court Circular announced that the Prime Minister, Clement Attlee, and the Leader of the Opposition, Winston Churchill, had formally agreed that as from that date, the honour had ceased to be political, and henceforth would be at the sovereign's personal disposal. This advice had, of course, been tended to George VI and accepted by him. Thus awards of the Garter today are always the personal choice of the Queen who, by the same agreement, may award the next senior order, that of the Thistle, as she sees fit.

Officers of the Order
The Sovereign
The Prelate (Bishop of Winchester, 'ex-officio')
The Chancellor
The Dean of Windsor
The Register

Garter King of Arms
The Gentleman Usher of the Black Rod
The Secretary

The chapel of the order is St George's Chapel at Windsor Castle. The original chapel built for Edward III was rebuilt in the reign of Edward IV, and was the Yorkist reply to the beautiful Lancastrian foundation of Eton College chapel by Henry VI. St George's Chapel marks the final flowering of the majesty of medieval Gothic architecture.

Ceremony of Investiture and Installation of New Knights

Except for detail, the ceremony of investiture and installation follows the same pattern for all the orders of chivalry—except the Royal Victorian Order and the Order of the British Empire which do not hold installation services and do not hang banners. It will not, therefore, be necessary to describe in detail more than this one ceremony of the Garter.

On the morning of the annual Garter Chapter and Service the Officers and Knights Companion assemble in the magnificent throne-room of Windsor Castle. The Queen's Bodyguard of the Yeomen of the Guard are posted round the throne and along the side walls, and everyone is in full state robes, regalia and uniform. The gilded roof and walls are decorated in splendid blazonry with the arms of former knights, and under the Canopy of State the steps of the throne are carpeted in blue, the colour of the Garter.

The Sovereign and her Consort having been escorted to their thrones Garter King of Arms, wearing for this one occasion not his herald's tabard but a scarlet mantle lined with white taffeta, is despatched with Black Rod to summon the candidate to the royal presence. Presently they return preceding the candidate who, wearing levée dress, or if he has military rank full-dress uniform, walks between his two knight sponsors. He kneels before the throne where the Sovereign bestows on him the accolade of knighthood. Then the gold and blue Garter is buckled round his left leg below the knee, and he is invested with Mantle, Collar, George and Hat. Finally he takes the oath of the order, which is administered to him by the Prelate.

The Installation

In pre-Reformation times the installation of new knights into their stalls followed High Mass celebrated in St George's Chapel. In modern times the installation follows lunch at Windsor Castle. A procession is formed, and the route is lined by dismounted troopers of the Household Cavalry wearing gleaming breast-plates and plumed helmets and with sabres drawn. These are stationed near the chapel, while Foot Guards line the earlier part of the route. The procession is headed by the Governor of Windsor Castle, who is followed by the Military Knights in their scarlet tunics. Next come the heralds and pursuivants of the College of Arms in their tabards, preceding the Knights Companion in mantle and hood and all wearing gold collars and plumed Garter hats; the new knights come first. At the end of the procession of knights walk the Chancellor and the Prelate, preceded by the Register and the Secretary. The Sovereign's procession which follows is headed by Garter King of Arms and the Gentleman Usher of the Black Rod, preceding Princes of the Blood and Her Majesty the Queen Mother. Finally, their trains of dark blue velvet mantles held by pages of honour in white knee-breeches and scarlet livery coats, walk the Sovereign and her Consort. The Yeomen of the Guard with their tall partisans bring up the rear of the Sovereign's procession.

State trumpeters sound a fanfare as the Sovereign mounts the steps at the West End to enter the Chapel. When all have taken their seats, each in his stall beneath his personal banner, the national anthem is sung. The Sovereign then commands:

'It is our pleasure that the Knight(s) Companion be installed'.

The new knight(s) is led by Garter King of Arms to his stall, and his banner is unfurled before him. Later it will be placed above his stall, there to remain until he dies.[5] The short service that follows concludes with a collect of thanksgiving for the founding of the order and the singing of the *Te Deum*.

Insignia of the Order

The Garter: Dark blue velvet 1in wide, edged with gold, and bearing in gold letters the words of the motto.

The Surcoat: Once a close-fitting tunic, this is now a broad sash of crimson velvet lined and edged with white taffeta, and worn attached to the hood on the right shoulder over the mantle and passing under it on the left side.

The Mantle: The most distinctive item of insignia, this mantle is of dark-blue velvet lined with white taffeta, and has a large representation of the central device of the star of the order embroidered on the left breast (on a shield argent a cross of St George surrounded by a gold-embroidered garter with buckle and motto).

The Hood: Once a full medieval hood with liripipe, this is now a crimson velvet casting hood attached to the right shoulder of the mantle.

Shoulder Knots and Cords: Attached to each shoulder of the mantle is a knot of white silk ribbon, sometimes known as 'Shoulder Knots of the Bath' (see Order of the Bath). The mantle is fastened by blue and gold tasselled cords.

The Hat: A black velvet Tudor hat with wide brim and lined with white taffeta. The hat is surmounted by a plume of white ostrich feathers with a tuft of black heron's feathers in the centre. The plume is fastened to the hat by a badge.

The Collar: This is made up of twenty-six buckled garters, each containing a red rose of enamel and alternating with knots of gold cord. With the George, the collar weighs 30 oz troy weight pure gold. The collar, with the George suspended from it, is worn over the mantle. On certain days it may be worn over full-dress uniform or court dress, but it is never worn when the riband of the order is worn.

The George: Worn pendent from the collar, the George is a gold and coloured enamel representation of St George in armour with spear in right hand slaying the Dragon.

The Badge: Known as 'The Lesser George', the badge of the order is a gold oval enclosing the same device as the George, but surrounded by the motto, wrought in the oval. It is worn on the right hip as a clasp for the ends of the riband.

The Star: This is an eight-pointed star of chipped silver in the centre of which is a cross of St George surrounded by a blue enamel garter bearing in gold the words of the motto. The star is always worn on the left breast on full-dress uniform, court dress or full evening dress coat.

The Riband: Introduced by Charles II, the colour is blue, and it is worn over the left shoulder to be secured on the right hip by the Lesser George. It is worn with full-dress uniform, court dress, or full evening dress *under* coat and waistcoat. The riband is never worn with the collar.

The later Stuart and Hanoverian princes seem to have worn the Garter Star (in the right position) pinned to a variety of dress. George IV, as Prince Regent, appears to have worn the star on an ordinary frock overcoat of the day when walking along the front at

Brighton. It is not, in the light of this knowledge, beyond the bounds of possibility that his august father, who insisted on 'God Save the King' being played by a small band on the beach at Weymouth every time he stepped from the royal bathing-machine into the water, wore the Garter Star on his bathing suit.

THE FOUNDER KNIGHTS OF THE ORDER OF THE GARTER

The Prelate	*Dean and Register*
The Bishop of Winchester	(John de la Chambre)
(William Edington)	

Sir Walter Paverley	Sanchet'd'Ambreticourt
Sir Henry Eams	Sir Otho Holland
Sir James Audley	Sir John Chandos
Sir Nele Loring	Sir Hugh Wrottesley
Sir Thomas Wale	Sir Miles Stapleton
Sir Richard FitzSimon	Sir John Grey
Sir Thomas Holland	Sir Hugh Courteney
John, Lord Mohun	Sir John Beauchamp
Sir Bartholomew Burghersshe	John, Lord Lisle of Rougemont
Roger, Lord Mortimer	William, Earl of Salisbury
Rafe, Lord Stafford	Captal de Buch
Thomas, Earl of Warwick	Henry, Earl of Lancaster

EDWARD, PRINCE OF WALES	KING EDWARD III
(The Black Prince)	(The Sovereign)

The Most Ancient and the Most Noble Order of the Thistle

Motto: '*Nemo Me Impune Lacessit*', ('No One Provokes Me With Impunity')

The origin of this order, the premier of Scotland, is obscure. The thistle was not adopted as the national badge until the reign of James IV (1488-1513), and there is no record of that cultured monarch founding

The Star *of the Order of the Thistle*

The Collar of the Order of the Thistle

an order of chivalry. An Order of Saint Andrew seems to have been founded in 1540 by James V, with himself as Sovereign together with twelve Knights Companion in imitation of Christ and the twelve apostles. But this order fell into abeyance when the Reformation came to Scotland, and no attempt was made to revive it because the Calvinist Protestant government believed all such knightly orders to be rooted in Popery. In 1687 James VII and II signed a royal warrant for 'the *restitution* of the Order of the Thistle', and whether or not the King was referring to James V's order by an alternative name, there is no doubt that this warrant, like that of the earlier Stuart king, expressly laid it down that the 'revived' order was to consist of James VII as Sovereign and twelve brethren knights 'symbolising Our Lord and the twelve apostles'. In fact, the patent of creation never passed under the Great Seal, no doubt because in the following year this Roman Catholic monarch was sent packing by his Protestant English subjects, and departed for good, incidentally sinking the Great Seal in the river Thames on his way. Before this happened, James had designated St Giles' Cathedral, Edinburgh, as the chapel of the order, and had appointed eight Knights Companion.

On 31 December 1702, Queen Anne issued a royal warrant reviving the Order of the Thistle with the same constitution as that provided by her royal father, and we may believe that this time the patent of creation did pass the Great Seal. The number of Knights Companion, however, remained eight until 120 years later when, in July 1821, George IV increased it to the twelve originally intended. This was during his famous progress through Scotland, the first British monarch to visit that country since James VII and II himself. In 1827 the number of knights was increased to sixteen, which is the number of creations allowed today, although, like the Garter, foreign royalty may be created honorary members. (The last such to be admitted was King Olav V of Norway in 1962.) In 1963, on relinquishing office as Prime Minister of the Commonwealth of Australia, Robert Menzies, as he then was, was created a Knight of the Thistle by the Queen.

Officers of the Order
The Sovereign
The Dean of St Giles
The Chancellor
The Lord Lyon King of Arms (Sovereign Head of the Scottish Court of Chivalry)

The Gentleman Usher of the Green Rod

The chapel of the order is St Giles' Cathedral, in Edinburgh, and the religious observances are according to the liturgy of the Presbyterian Church of Scotland.

Insignia of the Order

The Surcoat: Dark-blue velvet lined with white taffeta.

The Mantle: Dark-green velvet lined with white taffeta, and tied with green and gold tasselled cords. A large representation of the star of the order embroidered on the left shoulder of the mantle. Stitched to the summit of each shoulder are white silk ribbon knots ('Knots of the Bath').

The Hood: Dark-green velvet casting hood lined with white taffeta attached to the right shoulder of the mantle.

The Hat: Black velvet, Tudor style, with wide brim, but without plume.

The Collar: Gold with alternate devices of thistles and sprigs of rue enamelled in proper colours (the symbols of Picts and Scots).

The Badge: A gold figure of St Andrew carrying a white enamelled St Andrew's Cross, the whole surrounded by golden rays. The badge is always worn suspended from the collar.

The Star: A white enamelled St Andrew's Cross with gold rays displayed between the arms of the cross. At the centre, a green enamelled thistle on gold field surrounded by a green circlet bearing in gold letters the motto.

The star is worn on the left breast, under the same conditions obtaining for the Garter.

The Riband: Dark-green, this riband may not be worn with the collar—but, like the Garter, is worn over the left shoulder and fastened on the right hip by the badge as a clasp.

The Most Honourable Order of the Bath

Motto: *'Tria Juncta In Uno'* ('Three Joined in One')

Much confusion attends all attempts to prove a medieval date of foundation for this order. According to one school of thought, it was founded originally by Henry IV for the occasion of his coronation in 1399. Others hold that this monarch, far from founding a new order of chivalry, was in effect creating a large number of knights bachelor with a special investiture ceremonial invented to mark the occasion. It must not be forgotten that the term 'Knights of the Bath' was applicable to all knights bachelor not invested as knights of the sword (see above). What is certain is that, beginning with Henry IV, for over 250 years every succeeding monarch created in the Tower of London before his coronation a number of new knights as a mark of grace, and that these knights from an early date wore crimson mantles for the coronation and banquet at Westminster Hall immediately after. They were also given important feudal duties to carry out. Froissart has described the proceedings in 1399:

> The Saturday before his coronation he (Henry IV) departed from Westminster, and rode to the Tower of London with a great number; and that night all such esquires as should be made knights the next day, watched, who were the number of forty-six. Every esquire had his own bayne (bath) by himself; and the next day the Duke of Lancaster[6] made them all knights at the mass-time. Then had they long coats [mantles?] with strait sleeves, furred with mynever like prelates, with white laces hanging on their shoulders.[7]

Whatever its foundation, the 'Ancient Order' was discontinued after the coronation of Charles II, probably because this monarch was the last to practise the medieval custom of taking up residence at the Tower before coronation at Westminster.

The Modern Order of the Bath

By royal warrant dated 18 May 1725, George I 'revived' the Most Honourable Order of the Bath. The warrant laid it down that it should consist of the Sovereign and thirty-six knights companion, together with the officers of the order. A special feature of King George's creation is that it was to be a military order, creations being limited to officers of the Army and the Navy. The King himself, as is well-known, took little interest in English domestic matters; the inspiration and the detail were the work of Garter Anstis (see Chapter 1, on Heraldry), with the powerful support of Sir Robert Walpole, who was keen to have the new honour for himself (as 'Prime Minister', no doubt an exception to the 'military only' rule could be made in his case. Walpole also received the Garter in the next reign). There is a portrait in the possession of the Dean and Chapter of Westminster Abbey, painted by Canaletto, showing the procession of Knights of the Bath leaving the abbey with the Grand Master bringing up the rear. A curious feature the artist has preserved is the figure of the royal cook behind a chopping

The Star of the Order of the Bath

block and standing just within the great west door with cleaver in hand 'to strike off the spurs of unworthy knights'.

In 1815 the Prince Regent, to commemorate what he called 'the auspicious termination of the long and arduous contests in which the empire has been engaged', issued a new warrant enlarging the order to include three classes differing in ranks and degrees of dignity. In 1847 Queen Victoria extended membership to include civilians.

These classes, with the permitted numbers allowed (in 1970) in each class, are as follows:

Knights Grand Cross (GCB)	..	..	78	Military Division
Knights Commander (KCB)	..	..	191	
Companions (CB)	..	..	1055	

The same divisions obtain in the Civil section, where the numbers allowed in each class are (in 1970):

GCB	..	..	.. 25
KCB	..	..	.. 100
CB	..	..	.. 650

The Collar of the Order of the Bath

Officers of the Order

The Sovereign
The Great Master
The Dean of Westminster
The Bath King of Arms
The Registrar and Secretary
The Deputy Secretary
The Genealogist
The Gentleman Usher of the Scarlet Rod

The chapel of the order is the Henry VII Chapel in Westminster Abbey.

Insignia of the Order

(The right to wear mantle, hat and collar is restricted to the Knights Grand Cross)

The Surcoat: White satin.

The Mantle: Crimson satin lined with white taffeta. On the left side is embroidered a large representation of the star of the order.

The Hood: Crimson satin lined with white taffeta (a casting hood).

The Collar: Gold 30 oz troy weight. It is made up of nine imperial crowns, eight roses, thistles, shamrocks 'issuing from a gold sceptre', and enamelled in proper colours. These are linked by seventeen gold knots enamelled white.

The Badge (Military): A rose, a thistle, and a shamrock issuing from a sceptre between three imperial crowns, surrounded by the motto in gold letters on a red enamel field. The whole device is surrounded by a green enamel laurel wreath. At the base is a dark-blue enamel scroll bearing in gold letters the words "ICH DIEN".

The Badge (Civil): A gold oval containing the same device as the military badge, but surrounded by a gold band bearing the motto of the order.

The badge is normally worn suspended from the collar as in the Garter and the Thistle; but it may be worn on a narrow crimson riband round the neck when mantles and collars are not worn. Thus it is worn by those classes of the order not entitled to mantle and collar.

The Star (Military): A star with silver streamers on which is superimposed a gold Maltese Cross with the three imperial crowns of the badge. There are no other charges, but the motto surrounds the crowns, as on the badge.

The Star (Civil): A star of eight points silver with three imperial crowns at the centre surrounded by a red circlet bearing the motto. The star is worn on the left breast by both military and civil Knights Grand Cross, and by Knights Commander.

The Hat (GCB): Stiff black velvet with ostrich feather plume.

The Hat (Officers): Crimson velvet without plume. Since 1935 no hats have been worn by either Knights Grand Cross or Officers. Neither has the levée dress, which until that date was worn under mantles.

The Riband: Of crimson silk, it is worn over the right shoulder and secured on the left hip by the badge used as a clasp. The riband is never worn with the collar.

Knights Commander (Military and Civil)
This class of member does not wear either mantle or collar. The badge is smaller, but similar to that of GCB both divisions. The star for the military division is similar to that of GCB, but omits the gold Maltese Cross and is mounted on a silver cross patté, with rays. The civil star of this class is similar to the military, but the centre is as in the civil GCB.

Companions (Military and Civil)
This class of member has no star. A small badge, similar to the KCB badge, is worn by both divisions on a narrow crimson riband round the neck.

The Most Distinguished Order of St Michael and St George
Motto: '*Auspicium Melioris Avi*', ('Token of a Better Age')

This order of knighthood was founded on 27 April 1818 by the Prince Regent on behalf of his father, George III. The occasion was a curious one: it was intended to be an award of appreciation for services rendered to Great Britain by the Ionian Islands during the Napoleonic wars, these islands having been formed into an independent state under the protection of Britain in 1815. In the hundred years that followed, the order, which was constituted in three classes, was awarded to a variety of persons. Since the foundation of the Order of the British Empire in 1917, the Order of St Michael and St George has been awarded almost exclusively to diplomats and members of the British Foreign Service and Commonwealth Office.

This order is constituted in the following divisions or classes:
Knights or Dames Grand Cross (GCMG)
Knights or Dames Commander (KCMG or DCMG)
Companions (CMG)
Ladies have been admitted to this order since 1 January 1965.

Officers of the Order
The Sovereign
The Grand Master
The Prelate
The Chancellor
The Secretary

The Star of the Order of St Michael and St George

The Collar of the Order of St Michael and St George

The King of Arms
The Registrar
The Gentleman Usher of the Blue Rod
The Deputy Secretary
     The chapel of the order is in St Paul's Cathedral in London.

Insignia of the Order

(The right to wear mantle, hat and collar is restricted to Knights and Dames Grand Cross)

The Surcoat: None.

The Mantle: Saxon-blue satin lined with scarlet silk. A large representation of the star of the order is embroidered on the left side. The mantle is fastened with tasselled cords of gold, blue and scarlet; and white shoulder knots of the Bath adorn each shoulder.

The Hood: This is a casting hood of scarlet and blue.

The Hat: Blue satin lined with scarlet and surmounted by black and white ostrich feathers.

The Collar: Formerly gold, the collar is now of silver gilt. It is made up of alternating gold winged lions, enamelled Maltese Crosses, and the monograms 'S.G.' and 'S.M.' in gold. It is joined at the base by two facing gold-winged lions surmounted by a gold imperial crown.

The Badge: This is a white enamelled cross of seven arms and fourteen points surmounted by a gold imperial crown. The badge centre obverse shows on a red field a gold and enamel St Michael with flaming sword defeating Satan; the reverse depicts St George on horseback encountering the Dragon. The obverse centre is encircled by a blue band containing the motto in gold letters. The badge is worn by Knights and Dames Grand Cross suspended from the collar.

The Star: Seven silver rays with shorter gold rays between the silver rays, surmounted by a red enamelled cross of St George. Superimposed on the centre within a blue circle bearing the motto in gold is a larger representation of St Michael, as on the badge.

The star is worn on the left breast.

The Riband: This is 4-in wide Saxon-blue silk with a scarlet centre stripe. It is worn over the right shoulder and clasped with the badge on the left hip.

The riband is never worn with the collar.

No hats have been worn by Knights or Dames Grand Cross since the second world war. The under-dress is as for the Garter. Knights and Dames Commander receive no mantle, collar or riband. Instead they receive the star and the badge, but these are smaller though similar in design to those received by Knights and Dames Grand Cross. Companions receive only the smaller badge. KCMG, DCMG and CMG all wear their badge on a narrow riband of the order round the neck.

The Royal Victorian Order

Motto: 'Victoria'.

This order of chivalry was founded by royal letters patent of Queen Victoria dated 21 April 1896. Until 1948 (see above) this remained the only one of the nine British orders of chivalry whose award lay at the personal discretion of the Sovereign. The order is today constituted in five classes, all of which are bestowed for service to the monarch, or to members of the royal family. The Royal Victorian Order is open to both men and women. The five classes are:

Knights or Dames Grand Cross (GCVO)
Knights or Dames Commander (KCVO, or DCVO)
Commanders (CVO)
Members, Fourth Class (MVO)
Members, Fifth Class (MVO)
Silver-gilt Medal
Silver Medal
Bronze Medal

Officers of the Order

The Sovereign
The Grand Master (HM the Queen Mother)
The Chancellor (The Lord Chamberlain of the Household)
The Secretary (The Keeper of the Privy Purse)
The Registrar
The Chaplain
The chapel of the order is the Chapel of the Savoy in London.

Insignia of the Order

The Surcoat: Red satin.

The Mantle: Dark-blue silk edged with red satin and lined with white taffeta. A large representation of the star of the order is embroidered on the left shoulder. The mantle is fastened by dark-blue silk and gold tasselled cords. There are white shoulder knots of the Bath.

The Star of the Royal Victorian Order

The Collar of the Royal Victorian Order

The Collar: Gold with blue enamel octagonal pieces bearing ornate gold roses in the centre. The centre link is a gold medallion containing a round solid gold stamped effigy of the head of Queen Victoria crowned. On either side the octagonal pieces are linked in gold by the royal title in 1896, one word between the pieces:

VICTORIA-BRITT.-REG. DEF-IND-IMP.

The Badge: A white enamelled Maltese Cross of eight points, in whose centre is a crimson oval charged with the royal and imperial monogram of Queen Victoria in gold. The oval is encircled by a blue enamel band bearing the motto, and surmounted by a gold and red enamel imperial crown superimposed on the head of the cross. The badge is worn by GCVO suspended from the collar.

The Star: A star of eight points of chipped silver, with a replica of the badge at the centre. The star is worn on the left breast.

The Riband: Dark-blue silk with red and white edges. The riband is never worn with the collar of the order.

Knights and Dames Commander receive no mantle, collar or riband. They receive a star similar to that of the Grand Cross class, but smaller and of frosted silver. Knights Commander wear the smaller badge suspended from a narrow riband of the order's colours round the neck. Dames Commander wear their badge suspended from a bow of the order's riband colours on the left shoulder. Commanders do not have the star and regulations for wearing the badge are the same as for Knights and Dames Commander. Fourth and Fifth Class Members wear smaller badges with other medals on the left breast of the coat. The Fourth Class badge is of white enamel, and the Fifth Class badge of frosted silver.

The Most Excellent Order of the British Empire
Motto: 'For God and the Empire'.

The most recent foundation of British orders of chivalry, the Most Excellent Order of the British Empire was created by royal letters patent of George V dated 17 June 1917. The order was founded to reward those persons *other than military* who had rendered special service to the Empire; and its birth at a time when that empire was locked in a life and death struggle with the might of Germany and the Central Powers can be considered as a splendid gesture worthy of the ancient knightly code of chivalry. As it happened, the following year the constitution was amended to include a military division and, like the Victorian Order, it was to be open for awards to both men and women. Like that order, too, there were to be five classes. A peculiarity was that a distinction was made between awards for gallantry and awards for meritorious service. This distinction is marked in all classes of the order by the addition of a silver oak leaf for gallantry awards. There are, today, more awards made every year in the five classes of this order than in any of the other eight. Particularly is this the case in respect of the Officer and Member classes.

In this second half of the twentieth century the title of this latest of the orders of chivalry may sound somewhat ironic, and perhaps a case might be made for expanding the original title to read: 'The Most Excellent Order of the British Empire and Commonwealth', and the creation of a special class to be awarded by the Sovereign on the recommendation of those Commonwealth Prime Ministers whose countries ordinarily decline existing titles.

The five classes of this order, including two classes of members, are:
Knights or Dames Grand Cross (GBE)
Knights and Dames Commander (KBE and DBE)
Commanders (CBE)
Officers (OBE)
Members, Fourth and Fifth Class (MBE)

Officers of the Order
The Sovereign
The Grand Master
The Prelate (The Bishop of London)
The King of Arms
The Registrar
The Dean of St Paul's
The Secretary
The Gentleman Usher of the Purple Rod
The Prelate Emeritus
The Sub-Dean
The chapel of the order is in the crypt of St Paul's Cathedral, London.

Insignia of the Order
(The right to wear mantle, hat and collar is restricted to Knights and Dames Grand Cross)

The Star *of the Order of the British Empire, Knight Grand Cross*

The Collar *of the Order of the British Empire*

The Surcoat: None.

The Mantle: Rose-pink satin lined with grey silk. A representation of the star of the order is embroidered on the left side. The mantle is fastened by pearl-grey silk cords with pink and silver tassels. There are no shoulder knots.

The Hat: No hats have been worn since the second world war.

The Collar: This is entirely of gold. Alternate round medallions containing shields of the arms of England and the royal cypher are linked by lion's heads on either side of an imperial crown.

The Badge: A cross patonce enamelled pearl-grey surmounted by an imperial crown of gold. At the centre of the cross a round medallion of gold sculpted with the conjoint heads of King George V and Queen Mary facing dexter. The medallion is surrounded by a crimson circlet with the motto in gold letters.

The Star: This is a star of eight points with chipped silver rays. The centre is a larger representation of the badge centre.

The Riband: Rose-pink with two stripes of pearl-grey as borders (the military division riband has a further centre stripe of pearl-grey). Until 1937 the colour of the riband was purple. It was changed to its present colours in Coronation year. The under dress is as for the Garter, and the regulations for the wearing of insignia by Knights and Dames Commander, and for the lower classes of the order, are the same as for the Royal Victorian Order.

The Grand Priory in the British Realm of the Most Venerable Order of the Hospital of St John of Jerusalem

In its modern form this order was given its charter by Queen Victoria in May, 1888. The title, 'Venerable', was restored in 1926. Although Her Majesty the Queen is Sovereign Head of the British order, membership does not confer 'rank, title or precedence', and in this respect it differs fundamentally from all other orders of chivalry. There is a further difference: although the English Grand Priory has been a self-governing community since 1888, there is no denying that its origins are to be found in a far older Catholic order of military brethren whose governing body possessed sovereign rights entitling it to be represented by ambassadors at the courts of Christian kings. This ancient order also established Grand Priories in most of the countries of western Europe early in the middle ages, and was so represented in England until the Reformation. The titles still born by the officers of the modern British Priory bear witness to this ancient origin.

The Venerable Order of the Hospital of St John of Jerusalem has descended from a hospice dedicated to St John the Baptist and established at Jerusalem in the eleventh century for the relief of Christian pilgrims. When the Crusaders were forced to surrender the Latin kingdom to Saladin's Moslem armies in 1187, the monastic order administering the Jerusalem hospice became militarised, and at first concerned itself with the defence of the remaining Christian territories in Palestine and Syria. It was during this period of their existence that they built the great castles such as Krak des Chevaliers whose ruins are still so impressive. The knights took monastic vows, wore a black habit with a white cross, and in those early years they attracted to their ranks many noble-minded men. After the loss of these territories the Knights Hospitaller, as they had become known, retreated first to Cyprus, and then to Rhodes which they ruled as a sovereign power from 1309 until they were driven from the island by Sultan Souliman in 1522. During the long occupation of Rhodes the European Grand Priories, which had been set up as far back as the year 1100, not only continued their financial contributions to the maintenance of the Grand Magistracy in the island, but used their not inconsiderable influence in promoting another Crusade. It was not their fault that changed political circumstances in medieval Europe doomed such attempts to failure. When the order was forced to relinquish Rhodes it took possession of the island of Malta, over which it was given sovereign rights in 1522 by the Emperor Charles V. There it remained until 1798 when it was expelled by Napoleon. On the final defeat of Napoleon, Malta was retained by Great Britain, whose forces had captured the island, and there was to be no return of the order. Instead, the Grand Magistracy set up its headquarters in Rome where it has remained ever since.

The Grand Priory of England was dissolved along with all other monastic foundations by order of Henry VIII in 1539-40. The Scottish Priory suffered a like fate a few years later. Both institutions had played a not unimportant part in the life of each country. In England at the Reformation the total membership was about 120, distributed in 'commanderies' under 'preceptors', each answerable to the Grand Prior who lived at Clerkenwell in considerable state. He ranked as a baron and had been regularly summoned to Parliament with the abbots of the great Parliamentary abbeys. After the Reformation, religious intolerance and fears of Popery prevented any possibility of a revival for the next three centuries. But in 1827, on the eve of Catholic emancipation, the Knights Hospitaller of France, with the authority of the Grand Magistracy, lent their assistance to a revival in the British realm. In the event there was to be a Protestant revival, and it was to this that Queen Victoria gave her royal charter. The 1888 order was not recognised officially by the Grand Magistracy; such a course would not really have been possible in the light of Roman Catholic opinion at the time. Since the recent Vatican Council, Roman opinion has radically altered as regards relations with other faiths, and there is a real hope that in the not too distant future recognition may be accorded, and the English Grand Priory may once more take its place in the European and world community of the Knights Hospitaller. In 1945 a delegation of the Venerable Order in Great Britain paid an official visit to the Grand Master, Prince Chigi, at the Sovereign Order's headquarters in Rome. The excellent relationships established from that time resulted in a visit eighteen years later of the Sovereign Order's Grand Chancellor, His Excellency Don Enze di Napoli Rampolla, to St John's Gate, Clerkenwell where he was received with full ceremony by the Lord Prior, Lord Wakehurst. On Tuesday, 26 November 1963, a joint declaration was signed by the Lord Prior and the Grand Chancellor which, while involving no change in the constitutional independence of the two orders, recognised 'their historical links and the common tradition that inspires their humanitarian activities'.

The British order today conducts its business from the Chancery established at St John's Gate, Clerkenwell, London. This is actually the surviving gatehouse of the medieval priory destroyed in 1540. This business is mainly concerned with the maintenance of the order's three great foundations: the Ophthalmic Hospital in Jerusalem, the St John's Ambulance Association which is concerned with education in First Aid, and—its most widely known activity—the St John's Ambulance Brigade. The five classes of membership have the following titles:

Bailiffs and Dames Grand Cross
Knights and Dames of Justice and of Grace
Commanders
Officers
Serving Brothers and Sisters
Esquires

The Badge of the Order of the Hospital of St John of Jerusalem

Chaplains of the order take precedence between Knights and Esquires, and these ranks and titles, including the chaplains, preserve the religious temper of the original medieval priory.

Officers of the Order
The Sovereign Head (HM The Queen)
The Grand Prior (HRH The Duke of Gloucester)
The Lord Prior (Executive Head)
The Sub-Prior
The Titular Bailiff of Egle

Insignia of the Order

(The right to wear the mantle and riband is restricted to Bailiffs and Dames Grand Cross).

The Mantle: Black silk with the representation of the badge of the order embroidered in white silk embellished with gold on the left side. The mantle of the Grand Prior is of black velvet.

The Badge: A Maltese Cross of eight points in white enamel embellished between each of the four arms of the cross with a lion and a unicorn alternately, wrought in gold.

The Riband: Black watered silk.

The Star: A white enamelled star of eight points without embellishment, worn on the left breast.

The order has no collar. The badge is worn by Bailiffs and Dames Grand Cross on the left hip clasping the riband, which is worn over the right shoulder. Knights and Dames of Justice and of Grace wear the badge on a narrow black riband round the neck. Commanders wear their badge round the neck; but women Commanders wear it from a bow on the left breast. Officers wear the badge on the left breast, and Serving Brothers and Sisters wear a circular medal bearing the cross of the order in white enamel on a black enamel background. The embellishment of the badge for Third, Fourth and Fifth Class members is silver.

Regulations for the wearing of Insignia of Orders of Chivalry

Collars, badges, stars and ribands should be worn only with the dress set forth hereinafter:

Privy Councillor's lévee dress (knee-breeches or trousers)
Court dress (Court coat, waistcoat and knee-breeches)
Full evening dress
Full-dress military uniform (Review order or Blues for Army.
No 1 Dress for Royal Navy or Royal Air Force).

Not more than three neck badges, and not more than four stars, may be worn at any one time.

Collar Days: When it is appropriate to wear insignia on any of the dates listed below, the gold collar of the order must be worn in place of the riband. Collar and riband must never be worn at the same time.

1 January	New Year's Day
6 January	The Epiphany
6 February	The Queen's Accession Day
1 March	St David's Day
17 March	St Patrick's Day

25 March	Annunciation of the Blessed Virgin Mary
21 April	Birthday of HM The Queen
23 April	St George's Day
1 May	St Philip and St James's Day
29 May	Restoration of King Charles II
2 June	Anniversary of the Queen's Coronation
10 June	Birthday of HRH The Duke of Edinburgh
24 June	St John The Baptist's Day
29 June	St Peter and St Paul's Day
4 August	Birthday of HM the Queen Mother
29 September	Michaelmas Day
1 November	All Saints Day
30 November	St Andrew's Day
25 December	Christmas Day
Moveable Feasts:	Easter Sunday
	Ascension Day
	Whit Sunday
	Trinity Sunday
Special Occasions:	State Opening of Parliament
	Introduction of a Peer to the House of Lords
	Religious Chapters of the Orders of Chivalry

Some of the above dates, will of course, vary from reign to reign and others are applicable only during the lifetime of the members of the Royal Family so honoured.

6 CIVIC ROBES AND INSIGNIA

Historical Note

Not the least colourful of old English ceremonies are those still to be found surrounding the formal occasions of local government in towns of borough status. Details vary according to historical development, but civic robes and insignia still worn by mayors, sheriffs and aldermen, together with supporting officials, have their origin in medieval England when the principal cities won the right to conduct their own affairs independent of King or feudal lord. In Norman times the towns, including London, had paid tribute in the form of aids and service to the King direct, or in certain cases to a feudal tenant-in-chief to whom the privilege had been granted. But by the end of the twelfth century two new factors had arisen to modify profoundly the original set-up: increasing prosperity as the result of greatly extended trading had made it worthwhile for the King to seek the co-operation of the wealthy citizens; and the rise of the medieval guild was providing from the ranks of guild-master a class of citizen well qualified to conduct the government of the town's affairs. From this age dates the first of a series of royal charters conceding some measure of independence and self-government. Naturally, there was a price to be paid, and this usually took the form of a lump sum of money paid into the royal treasury. It is a mistake to believe that these twelfth- and early thirteenth-century charters bestowed complete independence. On the contrary, the influence of shire and baron's court often cut right across the hardly-won rights of the town commune. This is well illustrated by the civic history of London. And since the City rose to be the wealthiest and most splendid capital in Europe, a brief history of its rise to independence and the development of its civic ceremonial, which was to become the most magnificent of all cities', will serve as a model for all civic ceremonial. It is, of course, an historical fact that provincial towns were to copy to a greater or less degree what was done in this line in the City of London.

By the reign of Henry I (1100-35), London was divided into wards each in charge of an alderman who held a weekly husting to adjudicate over all kinds of civic business. This was not independence, since three times a year there was held the 'folkmoot' which corresponded to the provincial shire court and was, like the latter, presided over by the Sheriff of Middlesex, who was, of course, a royal officer. At the same time bishop, abbot and feudal magnate possessing property within the City walls were holding their own courts. Although Henry II severely curtailed the privileges of the feudal lords who, as a class, had reduced the realm to anarchy in Stephen's reign, his passion for law and order caused him to regard with suspicion any extension of civic liberty, and during his long reign the sheriffs of London were always royal nominees with extensive powers. After the death of this king, the burgesses eventually secured the right to elect two sheriffs who were each Sheriff of London and of Middlesex.[1] The royal approval, however, was still necessary to confirm these elections.

The first mention of a Mayor of London occurs in the year 1191 when we are told that the Commune of the City set up Henry Fitz-Ailwin to hold that office for life. It is perhaps worth noting that the title 'mayor' is derived from contemporary French; prior to the coming of the French kings of the house of Capet, France had been governed by officials acting in the name of the early Merovingian monarchs under the title 'mayor of the palace', and the title had come to signify a governor of a city or even of a province. It was during the period of office of Henry FitzAilwin that the mayor and aldermen of the City wards came to be recognised as the accepted governing body of London. Then, in 1215, one month before granting the famous charter at Runnymede, King John bestowed the first royal charter on the City. This not only confirmed all existing privileges, but also gave the citizens the right to elect their mayor annually. This was the theory in those early centuries, that the whole body of citizens had the privilege of choosing its rulers, and was applicable to provincial towns similarly blessed from this time on with charters.

By the thirteenth century, however, the government of most charter towns, including London, had become oligarchical. This came about because there was a natural tendency to place control in the hands of a rich property-owning class well qualified through experience in administration to exercise such control. There were no doubt many features which led to this situation, but certainly the most important was the influence of the great merchant guilds which arose at this period of history. The chief concern of the guilds was, of course, the regulation of trade and commerce; but their very nature and organisation provided them with the power to achieve a great deal more. Possessing a revenue derived from entrance fees and fines, possessing also an independent body of officials with an alderman at the head to carry out the guild's business, it can easily be seen how membership of guild and town borough tended to become identical; and the fact of such identification is borne out by the wording of many ancient charters.

It can, generally speaking, be said that during the later middle ages the common councils of London and other charter towns tended to be largely recruited from the ranks of guild-masters, particularly where the prosperity of these towns was very much the result of increased trade and commerce. Oligarchical control did not go unchallenged, and the social upheavals of the last half of the fourteenth century, triggered off by the Peasants' Revolt, led in many cases to a series of revolts by the general body of citizens against municipal control by the rich few. A particular point of dispute touched on the election of mayors and sheriffs. Details of the ceremonial processes involved in the City of London elections are described below; here it is only necessary to record that a number of these fourteenth-century disputes were settled by the issue of further charters by Henry IV and Henry V. No doubt the Lancastrian kings of the fifteenth century were conscious of the need to gain the support of the towns, and of London especially, in the light of their own weak dynastic claims. So it was that this century witnessed the final development of civic government which was to remain the norm until modern times.

A very important advance made at this time was the granting of county status to certain great towns. This had the effect of relieving the citizens of the obligation to attend the shire courts, which often met at a great distance from the particular town. As a result of this new status, mayor, sheriff and certain aldermen acquired the right to enquire into all transgressions and disturbances of the peace within their own territories. With such extended jurisdiction went the right to arrest felons and hold them in custody until the justices of gaol delivery (of whom the mayor was one) arrived to try the cases. These town courts were also now courts of records and granted authority to levy fines for licences of all kinds. We must now consider in more detail the office of mayor or Lord Mayor, the sheriffs, and the courts over which the former is called on to preside.

The Lord Mayor

The title 'Lord Mayor' is first found as 'dominus Maior' in the thirteenth century. The earliest recorded use of the English form, 'Lord Mair' occurs in the year 1414. It may not be without significance that this was the period during which Sir Richard Whittington was playing a not inconsiderable part in the affairs of the nation. This great and wealthy merchant, from around the year 1400, made a number of financial loans to the governments of both Henry IV and Henry V. He served four times as 'Lord Mayor' of London, the last in 1419, was for a short time a member of the royal council, and by his personal loans and influence assisted materially in effecting the victorious outcome of the warrior king's French expeditions. It may have been Whittington's membership of the Privy Council that secured for future Lord Mayors the title, 'Right Honourable', which they have borne ever since.

We have noted that the citizens of London had won the privilege of electing their mayor annually from King John, and that a hundred years later the election was practically confined to the ranks of the wealthier citizens, being mostly masters of the powerful livery guilds. By the beginning of the fifteenth century the rules governing the election of Lord Mayor and sheriffs had been standardised and remained as they are today. At an Assembly of the Liverymen and the Court of Aldermen, sitting in joint council presided over by the Lord Mayor, two names are put up by the liverymen to the Court of Aldermen, which then proceeds to make the final selection. An important condition of nomination is that the candidates should have served in the office of sheriff, and be aldermen of not less than five years standing. In the thirteenth century, both the election of the mayor and his admission to office took place on the same day, namely, 28 October, the feast of St Simon and St Jude. The day following he was presented to the Sovereign and the Barons of the Exchequer for the royal approval. In the absence of the Sovereign, presentation was before the High Constable of the Tower. Until 1751 admission to office and presentation before the Court of Exchequer continued to take place on 28 and 29 October respectively; but from 1347 and 1546 the election was put back to 13 October. In 1546, the day of the Lord Mayor's election was fixed for 29 September, the feast of St Michael and All Angels, as it remains today. The year 1751 witnessed the change from the old Julian to the Gregorian Calendar which had been in use in Europe since 1585. To ensure accuracy, this entailed the omission for that year of eleven days from the calendar with the result that 28 October (O.S.) was followed by 9 November (N.S.). This is the reason why the famous annual procession through the streets of London to the Law Courts in the Strand for presentation before Her Majesty's judges, representing the Sovereign, has continued to take place on 9 November. And, until after the second world war, all provincial mayors took office on the same day.

Of recent years, the procession through the streets of London has been displaced to the nearest Saturday in the interests of avoiding disruption of traffic, and the Lord Mayor's Banquet in Guildhall, which formerly took place the same day as presentation at the Law Courts, is now held on the Monday following the Saturday of the procession.

A point of historical interest is that, in early days, new Lord Mayors rode on horseback through the City streets to Westminster for their presentation before the Court of Exchequer. Later still, they made this journey up the Thames by state barge to land at the Privy Council steps for Westminster Hall, where the royal judges held their courts until the reform of the judiciary in 1872.

The Sheriffs

The office of sheriff is of greater antiquity than that of mayor. The word is derived from the Saxon 'shire reeve', meaning roughly executive officer or magistrate for the county. The sheriff was always a royal nominee, and in Norman and early Plantagenet times always appointed from the knight class. Among his duties was that of presiding over the shire moot. Also, as the King's chief officer for the county, he collected the portion of fines and feudal dues apportioned to the Crown. He had powers of arrest, and was required to keep in custody all those whom the law required to be delivered up to the justices of oyer and terminer in general gaol delivery. Finally, the sheriff was responsible for the selection of juries and for carrying out executions and other punishments inflicted by the royal courts. For the most part, the medieval sheriffs were a hard-working and loyal body of royal officials, without whose faithful service the day to day government of the country could not have been carried on. One may take it that the traditional figure of the Sheriff of Nottingham of the Robin Hood legends is an exception to the rule.

Alone among the counties and 'county status' towns of England, the City of London is unique in possessing two sheriffs, and in possessing the right to elect them. In 1132, Henry I had granted the City the right to choose its own justiciar, or chief royal officer, to represent the King. In 1199, London was granted the privilege of electing two sheriffs, of London and Middlesex, each officer to represent these territories jointly, and this double office was held by all London sheriffs until the passing of the Local Government Act of 1888. Since that date, although London has continued to elect annually two sheriffs, both have represented the City only. Like their provincial fellow sheriffs, their modern duties have been severely curtailed, but they still attend judges on circuit, execute both the civil and criminal judgements of the courts of justice, and—one of their most important functions— summon juries for the various courts within their jurisdiction. In London, the two sheriffs constantly attend the Lord Mayor when he presides in state over the Court of Aldermen, Common Council and on every ceremonial occasion.

The Court of Aldermen

The word 'alderman' is derived from the late Saxon 'earldorman' which signified a representative of the royal government in the shire. In fact, the alderman presided over the shire court until the sheriff came to supersede him. In London in early days, the office of alderman was generally hereditary and the holders of the office were expected to have a good knowledge of the law and to execute it. The division of the City into 'wards' goes back to a very early date, and it became the custom for an alderman to preside over each ward. The conduct of their wards was managed in what were called 'wardmoots'. There is no need to follow the development of the system through the middle ages except to note that at some time the hereditary principle was replaced by an electoral one. Today, there are twenty-six aldermen representing twenty-six wards, and these aldermen, who sitting together constitute the Court of Aldermen, are elected for life by the freemen and liverymen of the wards who collectively constitute the Court of Common Council. It has already been stated that it is from the ranks of the aldermen that the Lord Mayor is chosen.

The Court of Common Council

This court is elected by the body of freemen and liverymen of the City for one year. The liverymen are members of some seventy-five companies (Grocers' Company, Goldsmiths' Company, etc) which are descended from the medieval guilds. A ratepayer may become a member of a company by personal application and the payment of a small subscription. This makes him a 'freeman'. By payment of a rather large subscription he may become a 'liveryman' with the right to wear the livery or uniform of his company. Two hundred and six liverymen are elected annually to sit with the twenty-six aldermen under the Lord Mayor and sheriffs, and this 'Common Council' constitutes the Corporation, or government, of the City of London.

Court of Common Hall
This is an assembly of the freemen, liverymen and municipal officers, whose responsibilities are of an elective nature only.

Officers of the City of London
There are a number of municipal officers of the City of London who are called upon to perform duties which range from legal to purely ceremonial. Most of these are, strictly-speaking, officers of the Corporation; but there are three officers who belong directly to the Lord Mayor's household. These are, in order of seniority of creation of office: the Common Cryer and Sergeant-at-Arms, the Sword Bearer, and the City Marshal. These officials in the household come under the authority of the Lord Mayor's secretary for administrative purposes.

Common Cryer
This is the most ancient office in the Lord Mayor's household. It seems to have been well-established before 1338, when there is reference to this official. It would appear that in that century the office was filled by one of the King's sergeants-at-arms. In 1419 there is reference to the 'Sergeant-at-Arms of the City or Common Cryer', and in 1518 we learn that he wore a ceremonial gown, but unfortunately no details have survived.

The Common Cryer's duties today are mainly concerned with carrying the Great Mace of the City before the Lord Mayor. He has also acquired the duty of proclaiming the Dissolution of Parliament from the steps of the Royal Exchange, where he is attended by state trumpeters and City beadles.

Sword Bearer
This official is first heard of in the sixteenth century. He carries the City Sword before the Lord Mayor on ceremonial occasions. Costumes and robes of these officials will be described in the next section; but it can

The City of London's Sword-Bearer with Sword of State

be noted here that this official's distinctive fur hat is taken off and placed with the sword on the table before the Lord Mayor when he takes his seat in sessions, of the Court of Aldermen and Common Council.

City Marshal
In the year 1595 royal letters patent of Elizabeth I gave authority to the Corporation of London to appoint a marshal to maintain order in the

The City Marshal, whose office dates back to 1595

City. At this period of English history, and for most of the following century, the City Marshal's job cannot have been a sinecure, for rioting by the City apprentices and the riff-raff was a recurring hazard in an age less disciplined than ours and, of course, lacking a police force. It is therefore perhaps not very surprising that the passing of the Metropolitan Police Acts of 1829 and 1839 removed many of his responsibilities from this official.

Today, the City Marshal's duties are concerned largely with the marshalling of civic processions within the City of London, and the calling of names of officials in the proper order of precedence. His function most often seen by the general public is that of challenging in the Lord Mayor's name bodies of troops exercising their privilege of marching through the City. The Marshal also challenges the Officers of Arms seeking permission to enter the City to make proclamation.

Origins of Civic Robes

Robes of dignity for city officials may well have developed out of liveries adopted by certain medieval guilds, but this is not known for certain. The close connection between the craft guilds of the middle ages and mayor and aldermen has already been noted, and a constant feature of town life in those early days was the great guild festival when mayor and aldermen joined with guild-masters and other officials in procession to church on the annual feast of the patron saint. This would naturally be an occasion for splendid displays of pageantry such as our medieval forbears delighted in, the splendour of such processions not only enhancing the dignity and importance of the chief citizens taking part, but also being regarded by the ordinary townspeople as a source of legitimate pride in their city's wealth and importance. Originally, the wearing of a distinctive dress by the members of a particular guild must have been a matter of domestic concern reflecting the wealth and importance of the guild, much in the same way that the wearing of gold chains round the neck became the recognised symbol of wealth among the merchant class and not specifically the insignia of a royal order or office. The fact that many of the greater crafts in the more important towns of England had, by 1370, come to possess royal charters granting them special powers to regulate their several trades, would have given added reason for these guilds to adopt special liveries to be worn on public occasions. Such charters before the end of the fourteenth century had been granted in London to the goldsmiths, the skinners, the tailors, the girdlers, the drapers, the vintners and the fishmongers' companies. These were the great livery companies and, as the name suggests, a special dress or 'livery' was worn on all ceremonial occasions. By the middle of the fifteenth century this special livery had come to be confined to the more prominent members of each guild, and it is recorded that in the year 1475 attendance at the elective assembly of the City of London, called 'common hall', was limited to the City Common Council and freemen *wearing liveries*. Thus the wearing of distinctive livery had come to signify not only wealth but political power.

Such was the early history of livery, which probably took the form of a furred long gown worn over the contemporary long robe of dignity. It seems likely that there was little attempt to standardise colour in the earlier days, though green, black velvet and murrey were fashionable colours. It is even possible that City officials, such as mayor, sheriff and aldermen, originally wore the livery of their particular guilds since, as we have seen, these officials were usually recruited from the senior ranks of the livery companies. But by 1415 there is evidence to suggest that special robes were being worn on the most solemn occasions by the City magistrates. In that very year Henry V, on his triumphant return from Agincourt, was received by the Lord Mayor and aldermen of London who were all robed in scarlet. Four years later the chronicles record that, at the election of a new Lord Mayor, violet robes were worn. No doubt throughout the fifteenth century and in early Tudor times colour was not standardised, though edging and lining were most likely furred in squirrel, fur being a symbol of dignity and wealth in the middle ages.[2] It was not until the year 1568 that the first Ceremonial Book of the City of London was printed, and we learn from it that gowns and cloaks of aldermen and certain other officials were to be fur-trimmed and lined, and black, scarlet or violet 'according to season'. The mayor was to wear crimson velvet and a gold collar of 'SS', and was to carry the City Sceptre. Very little further change has taken place except to extend the range of gowns to other City officials and to standardise the gowns of liverymen. Today, the Lord Mayor of London has six gowns:

> Black fur-trimmed
> Scarlet fur-trimmed
> Violet fur-trimmed
> Black and gold damask
> Crimson velvet reception robe (similar to peer's investiture robe)
> Crimson velvet robe for coronations.

Aldermen and sheriffs have robes of scarlet, violet and black. Common Counsellors (liverymen) wear at all times gowns of mazarine blue.

In the provinces, Lord Mayors normally have two gowns: scarlet fur-trimmed, and black and gold damask; while mayors have the scarlet fur-trimmed robe only. The colour and style of provincial aldermen and counsellors' gowns vary; but violet for aldermen and blue for counsellors seem to be favourite colours.

Insignia

The figure of the mace-bearer, walking before the mayor with a great silver-gilt mace borne on his shoulder, is familiar to thousands of citizens in the towns of England and Wales which support the dignity of mayor and corporation. Almost as noteworthy is the gold chain of office and pendent badge worn by mayors with and sometimes without their robes. Both these items of insignia find their place, as we have noted, in state ceremonial, too. The City of London is unique in possessing no less than seven principal ornaments of civic insignia, excluding the collars or chains of office worn by Lord Mayor and sheriffs. These, the Crystal Sceptre, the Great Mace, the Pearl Sword, the Sword of State, the Black Mourning Sword, the Old Bailey Sword and the City Purse, will be described in detail.

The Great Mace
As has been noted elsewhere, the mace is a very ancient symbol of authority. In its origins it was an iron club, weighted at the business end and grooved or spiked for greater effect, to be employed by mounted knights to unseat their opponents in battle and tournament. No doubt the effectiveness of this weapon as an instrument of war suggested its adoption as a fitting symbol of royal, and later civic, authority second only in importance to the sword. The fact that in its ceremonial use the war head and holding end have been reversed may possibly be explained by the theory that what was once a weapon and a military emblem had become an emblem of domestic (royal) authority. Thus, in fact, the club end dwindled to become the holding knob of today, while the former holding knob has developed into the elaborate chased and carved gilt crown with which everyone is familiar. Certainly, the Great Mace represents royal authority, whether exercised by Parliament or Lord Mayor. That is why in the presence of the Sovereign all maces are covered (the House of Commons mace is left outside the door of the Lords when the Speaker goes to the Bar of that House to face the Sovereign or Her Lords Commissioner).

The Corporation of London has more than one mace. These are the smaller maces carried by the sergeants-at-arms. The number of such maces and their sergeant bearers has varied through the centuries. In 1354 Edward III confirmed the prescriptive right of sergeants to carry gilt or silver maces before the mayor. As far back as 1244 authority had been given for staves to be borne before the chief magistrate. Through the centuries the number of these small maces varied between two and eight, with their attendant bearers. Today there are two Sergeants-at-Mace, one for duty with the sheriffs, and the other for duty at the Lord Mayor's court. The City Great Mace was certainly in existence before the year 1338. We have no means of knowing what this mace looked like, for a new one was made in 1559 at the very beginning of Elizabeth's reign. There was a second replacement in 1660—this latter may well have been because, during the period of the Commonwealth, the old 1559 mace had been replaced by a more republican symbol. The Great Mace carried before the Lord Mayor today and placed on the table before him in Guildhall was made in 1735 and is of silver gilt. It is 5ft 3in long and weighs 304oz.

The Crystal Sceptre

This precious and ancient article of the Corporation of the City of London's insignia is always in the charge of the City Chamberlain and is handed to every new Lord Mayor by his predecessor on taking office. Thereafter it is only carried in procession when the sovereign is present, and by the Lord Mayor himself on the rare occasion of a coronation.

The first mention in the records of the Crystal Sceptre is for the year 1504, when it is recorded that it was carried at the funeral procession of Elizabeth of York, the consort of Henry VII. But the evidence is that at least the shaft dates from Saxon times, though the head may be fifteenth century. The whole sceptre is 18in long, and the crystal shaft is in two sections divided by knobs of crystal set in gold.

The City Swords

It is not known when the privilege of having a sword carried before him was first granted to a mayor. The earliest written record is of permission being granted to a mayor of Coventry to have one sword borne before him in the year 1388. It would follow almost certainly that the mayors of London must have been granted this privilege even earlier. As has already been mentioned, the City of London possesses no less than five swords, and these are, as follows:

The Pearl Sword

This sword dates from the year 1571, having been presented to the Lord Mayor and Corporation by Elizabeth I on the occasion of her opening of the first Royal Exchange. The Pearl Sword is 3ft 11in long and is encased in a scabbard which is pearl encrusted. It is carried immediately before the Lord Mayor on great ceremonial occasions. This is also the sword which the Lord Mayor presents for the Sovereign to touch at the City boundary when the monarch enters the City of London.

The Sword of State

There has survived no written record of the origin of this sword, but it is believed to date from around the year 1680. This is the sword normally borne before the Lord Mayor and placed on the table when Common Council is in session, the Mayor presiding. It is 4ft 3in long. The pommel is of silver-gilt wrought with allegorical figures of Justice and Fame. The scabbard is covered in red velvet adorned with silver gilt lockets.

The Black Mourning Sword

An ordinance of 1534 refers to the purchase of a sword with black velvet sheath, and we can take this as the first reference to a City Mourning Sword. The present sword is 4ft 2½in long. The hilt and guard are of iron japanned black, while the grip and the scabbard are covered in black velvet. This sword is carried ceremonially for state funerals and for mourning the death of any member of the royal family.

The Old Bailey Sword

This sword, unlike those previously described, is not carried, but is fixed above the Lord Mayor's central seat on the Bench of the Central Criminal Court to remind all that as First Commissioner of Justice he takes precedence in the City over all judges and even over the Lord Chancellor. The sword, which is 3ft 11¼in long, dates from the sixteenth century, but there are later additions. The hilt has a round pommel of copper gilt wrapped with silver wire, and the scabbard is covered with purple velvet decorated.

The Mansion House Justice Room Sword

This sword, like the Old Bailey Sword, is a fixed one.

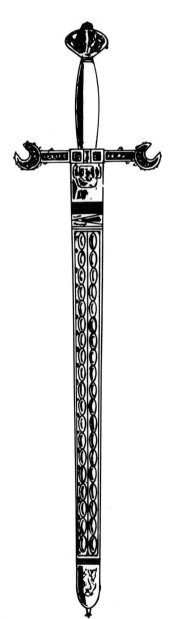

The Pearl Sword of the City of London

The City Purse

This is a bag, measuring 10½in by 9½in, made of red cloth-of-gold embroidered on both sides with gold scrolls and leaf-work together with the City arms worked in silver thread. The purse is lined with red silk. Its opening is drawn closed by cords having red and gold tassels decorated with pendent knobs of red and gold. It is in the charge of the City Chamberlain. In origin, it may date from the reign of Elizabeth I, or early seventeenth century, and was probably used to contain the mayoral seal. Ceremonially today it is one of the items of insignia handed over to the new Lord Mayor on taking office, and symbolically represents the balance of money held by the Corporation and handed over to the charge of the new Lord Mayor.

The Mayoralty Seal

A common seal for the Corporation of the City of London must have been granted soon after King John's charter granting a measure of local government, because among an overwhelmingly illiterate population the affixing of official seals was the only outward sign of authenticity. There is no extant record, however, of an early seal or seals. The first direct reference is in 1381 when it is recorded that the mayoralty seal for the City of London was broken and destroyed as being 'too rude and ancient' for the increasing dignity of the capital. A new seal was then made bearing the earliest representation in existence of the City arms. This seal remained in use for over five hundred years. In 1912 this ancient seal was placed in the City Museum where it may still be inspected. The new seal in use today is practically a copy of the old one. It is the only seal handed over physically to the new Lord Mayor at the ceremony of his admission to office. The museum seal is 2¼in in diameter. The obverse shows the two figures of St Paul (patron saint of London) and St Thomas Becket (the martyred archbishop who was a Londoner); the former figure holds an uplifted sword, while the latter is shown mitred. Below is a representation of the Blessed Virgin and Child. The City arms are represented on the reverse side.

Lord Mayor's Personal Insignia

Collar, or Chain of Office

The personal insignia of office of all lord mayors and mayors of England and Wales is the 'chain of office' and badge. Both chain and badge in the provincial boroughs follow a style and pattern dictated by local custom. In the City of London the chain is a Collar of 'SS'. The origins and description of this collar have been set down in an earlier chapter. Today, the only other persons entitled to wear this ancient article of insignia are the Lord Chief Justice and officers of the College of Arms. The collar is worn by the Lord Mayor of London whenever he wears his robes. Certain provincial mayors wear their collars or chains on some occasions over morning dress or lounge suits.

The Badge of Office

The Lord Mayor of London wears the Badge of Office on all public occasions. In plain morning dress or evening dress, he wears it suspended from a dark-blue silk riband round the neck. On state and civic occasions, when wearing robes, the badge is worn suspended from the Collar of "SS".

The present Badge, or Jewel as it is sometimes called, was made in 1802 and reset in 1866. It replaced earlier badges or jewels of 1588 and 1607. It consists of a sardonyx set in gold on which is carved out the City arms enclosed in a garter of gold and dark blue enamel bordered with rose-cut diamonds and bearing the City's motto, 'Domine Dirige Nos', also in rose diamonds. Around the whole is a wreath of roses with thistles and shamrocks intertwined composed of 219 brilliants and 24 rose-cut diamonds. Truly a fitting 'jewel' for the chief magistrate of the financial centre of the world.

The Sheriffs' Chains of Office

During their year's term of office the two City sheriffs wear over their gowns chains of office with pendent badges. These are much less magnificent than badge and collar of the Lord Mayor. The sheriffs' chains are linked chains of gold in three strands, the links formed of the City arms, which is also embodied in the badge. Unlike the history of the Lord Mayor's insignia, these are more personal, the custom being for each sheriff to have his chain and badge presented to him by the liverymen and freemen of his ward.

In the provinces there is no sheriff of borough towns, only the High Sheriff of the county, whose authority with regard to the summoning of juries and the carrying out of executions and certain punishments of felons extends to towns within his county jurisdiction.

Civic Robes and Uniforms

It has been noted that the Lord Mayor of London has no less than six ceremonial robes or gowns. The sheriffs and aldermen have three, and the liverymen one only. These will now be described in more detail, with a short list of the ceremonial occasions when each is worn.

The Black and Gold robe (entertaining gown) of the Lord Mayor of London

Robes of the Lord Mayor

The Scarlet Robe: Trimmed with squirrel fur, it is faced with a broad black velvet band running down the front on both sides of the centre opening and extending round the wide sleeves of the gown. These black bands are known as 'guards' and figure also on the scarlet gowns of sheriffs and aldermen. This robe is worn for the procession of the new Lord Mayor to the Law Courts to be presented before Her Majesty's judges (Lord Mayor's Day); at Sessions Court on Red Letter Days (see Chapter 4, on Legal Dress); when presiding over Court of Aldermen on Common Council, and on all other occasions when one or other of the other gowns are not directed to be worn.

The Violet Robe: This robe, also furred and similar in design to the scarlet robe, is worn by the new Lord Mayor for the ceremony of Presentation to the Lord Chancellor on his taking office; for the ceremony of the Admission of the Lord Mayor-elect at Guildhall; for presiding at Sessions Court (except on Red Letter Days); and for the ceremony of Admission of the Sheriffs to office.

The Black Robe: This is a plain black gown and is worn only on fast days for services at St Paul's Cathedral.

The Black and Gold Robe (Entertaining Gown): This is a magnificent robe of black damask, velvet and gold lace, with square collar somewhat resembling a Chancellor's robe. A broad gold band extends right down the two edges of the front opening. It is worn for the traditional banquet given by the new Lord Mayor in honour of his predecessor in office; for the State Dinner given to Her Majesty's judges; for the Fruiterers' Company Dinner; on Hospital Sunday; for the traditional sermon at St Paul's Cathedral on the first Sunday of the Trinity Law sittings; and for the ceremony of Presentation of Honorary Freedom of the City.

The Crimson Velvet Reception Robe: This splendid robe is indistinguishable from the investiture or coronation robe of an earl. It is of crimson velvet lined and edged with fur of miniver, and has a miniver hood spotted with ermine tails in bars numbering three, as for an earl. The opening is down the middle of the front. The robe is worn for the ceremony of Presentation of the City Sword to the Sovereign; at Guildhall for the Address to Head of a Foreign State; and for a solemn Service of Thanksgiving at St Paul's Cathedral. (See colour illustration, p. 88.)

The Special Crimson Velvet Robe: This magnificent robe is very rarely seen by the public, for the excellent reason that it is worn by the Lord Mayor only at a coronation ceremony in Westminster Abbey. The robe is thus likely to be worn only once in a lifetime—the last Lord Mayor of London to put on this vesture was Sir Rupert de la Bere, Lord Mayor 1952-53, for the coronation of Queen Elizabeth II. It is a long, ankle-length robe with a front opening faced with broad miniver bars running latitudinally across the front on both sides.

The robes of a Sheriff of the City of London

Robes of Sheriffs and Aldermen

These officials have three gowns: scarlet, violet and black; and they are identical with similar robes worn by the Lord Mayor. The occasions on which each is worn are as follows:

The Violet Robe: For the ceremony of Presentation of Lord Mayor to the Lord Chancellor; for the ceremony of Admission of Lord Mayor-elect; at Sessions of Court (except Red Letter Days); St Thomas's Day Wardmote; the ceremony for the election of sheriffs on St John Baptist Day (24 June); the ceremony of Admission of Sheriffs to Office (for this ceremony the sheriffs themselves wear their scarlet gowns).

The Black Robe: For fast-day services at St Paul's Cathedral.

The Scarlet Robe: This is worn for all civic ceremonies other than those named above.

Ceremonial Hats

The Lord Mayor and all aldermen 'who have passed the Chair', ie, who have held the office of Lord Mayor, wear a tricorn embellished with black feathers. The sheriffs and the aldermen who 'have not passed the Chair' wear black cocked hats.

NOTES

Notes to Chapter 1

1 The correct pronunciation of this name in the sixteenth century is not known. In a recent television serial, 'The Six Wives of Henry VIII', the Lord Chancellor of that name was addressed as 'Wrottesley'. This is surely wrong in the light of the derivation 'Writhe'. Other authorities have proposed 'Wroseley', but it is possible that Professor A. L. Rowse comes nearest with his suggestion of 'Risley'.

2 See note 1 above.

3 The portrait of Henry VI in the National Portrait Gallery in London shows this monarch wearing a gold collar in which single gold letter 'S's' are separated by a series of other emblems.

4 In actual fact Wolsey surrendered the Great Seal to the Master of the Rolls (Dr John Taylor) in the presence of the Dukes of Norfolk and Suffolk at York Place (later renamed Whitehall) on Monday, 18 October 1529. It is not recorded that he surrendered also a Collar of 'SS'.

Notes to Chapter 2

1 The Roman Catholic Pontifical requires that all the sacramental oils for the ensuing year must be blessed by the bishop of the diocese or his coadjuter after Mass on Maundy Thursday.

2 A long, white linen garment reaching to the feet and very similar to the alb worn by bishop and priest beneath chasuble and dalmatic.

3 Catholic bishops and archbishops ceremonially wear three kinds of mitres, plain white for requiems and funerals, the jewelled mitre and the gold mitre. The Pontifical requires both jewelled and gold mitres to be worn at certain parts of the Mass when the bishop pontificates.

Notes to Chapter 3

1 Before the passing of the Parliament Act (1911), all the diocesan bishops of the two English provinces sat in the Lords. In actual numbers they did not exceed today's total, since the various modern dioceses had not then been created. Until the dissolution

of the monasteries (1536-40) some twenty-five abbots representing the great Parliamentary abbeys also received writs of summons, as did the Grand Prior of the Order of St John of Jerusalem.

2   All Scottish peers who can prove that their barony carries a writ of summons may now attend and vote in the Lords. Until legislation embodied in the Parliament Act of 1947, at a dissolution of Parliament the peers of Scotland met at the palace of Holyrood House to elect thirty of their number to represent them in the United Kingdom Parliament.

3   No new Irish peers have been created this century. Since 1922 Irish peers have lost the right to a writ of summons unless they had been receiving the writ before separation took place with the creation of the Irish Free State. There are now (1971) none still sitting. Irish peers inheriting their titles may, however, exercise the privilege of Privy Councillors not members of the House of Lords and listen to debates in the chamber 'from the steps of the throne'. This privilege is also shared with the eldest sons of the peers entitled to sit and vote.

4   In pre-Reformation times the Chancellor was always a bishop or archbishop (see Chapter 4).

5   No record of any ceremony connected with creation or investiture has survived. Richard, Earl of Cornwall, was elected 'King of the Romans', the title given to the prospective heir of the Holy Roman Emperor. It may well be that Henry III bestowed the dukedom on his brother to mark his elevation on the Continent. It may also be significant that this title has for centuries been assumed at birth by the eldest sons of English monarchs.

6   The Irish title was probably given to avoid offending the susceptabilities of those English peers who hated de Vere as a King's favourite. As Marquess of Dublin he seems, however, to have sat 'between the dukes and earls' in Parliament.

7   Investiture with the sword remained an essential item of symbolic ceremonial for all degrees from that of earl upward.

8   No reason is given for this. A possible explanation is that the Duke of Somerset, as Lord Protector for the young King Edward VI, hoped by persuading the monarch to grant this signal mark of distinction to enlist the support of the new peers for his usurpation of power. It may not be without significance that the extension of such ornaments to other degrees of peerage followed the coronations of James I and Charles II.

9   It is not unreasonable to assume that the appearance of these robes in the fifteenth century owed much to the personal intervention of Edward IV, whose policy it was not only to make his

court a centre of power and magnificence such as it had not been before, but also to attract to that court a feudal peerage whom events over the passed thirty years had showed it was dangerous to leave in isolation on their estates. It is also known that this monarch was at pains to encourage by every means possible England's profitable wool trade, and the clothing of the chief men of the realm in fine scarlet wool when the estates of the realm assembled before his throne may be regarded as a fine piece of advertising.

10   Sir Thomas Butler, Resident Governor of the Tower of London and Keeper of the Jewel House, states that the 'Cap of Estate' was a badge of rank first worn by Edward III, and that it sometimes took the place of the royal crown. He goes on to state that it was Henry VII who introduced the custom of wearing his crown on top of this cap 'presumably for greater comfort'. If this is correct, and there is no reason to doubt the authority of Sir Thomas for reasons that must be obvious, then the royal custom seems to have predated that followed by the peers by two hundred years.

11   By ancient tradition all peers of the realm are formally addressed by the Sovereign as 'cousin', no doubt symbolising the close relationship in early feudal times between the great tenants-in-chief and their King.

Notes to Chapter 4

1   Star Chamber, or 'Camera Stellaris', most probably received its famous name from the small hall or apartment in the old royal palace of Westminster where the Privy Council customarily held its meetings from the time of Edward IV. This palace was destroyed by fire (except Westminster Hall) in the reign of Henry VIII, but either the old ceiling decorated with stars was recreated at Whitehall or St James or, as some early prints seem to suggest, the old hall escaped destruction in the fire.

2   At first sight it would appear that the Treasurer must have been usurping the function of the Lord Chief Baron. But the former, as a great officer of state with ultimate responsibility for the realm's finances, might well preside over a full bench when a question of taxation or fiscal policy was before the court. The office ceased to exist when Charles, Duke of Shrewsbury, resigned in October 1714. Since that date a commission has performed the duties, and it is not without significance that since Sir Robert Walpole took office as George I's chief minister in 1722, every 'prime minister' has taken the oath as 'First Lord

of the Commission for executing the Office of Lord High Treasurer'.

3 In modern times the mantle is worn with the miniver on the outside.

4 The Lord Chancellor also presides over the Judicial Committee of the Privy Council, which is the supreme court 'to advise Her Majesty' on appeals from the supreme courts of the British dominions and colonies overseas. Rather naturally, its work is not so extensive as it once was. The committee also acts as the ultimate court of appeal in matters ecclesiastical for the Church of England. This side of its activities may be explained by the fact that, in law, the monarch is, by the Act of Uniformity 1662, 'Supreme Governor of the Church of England'.

5 It is sometimes forgotten that, in the middle ages, it was not so much a case of kings choosing their chief ministers from the ranks of the higher clergy, as of kings rewarding a highly professional class of servant by the gift of bishoprics whose feudal revenues might be expected to support them in the style of living contemporary custom dictated. These political bishops were, of necessity, seldom resident in their diocese.

Notes to Chapter 5

1 Today there are only three resident Canons of Windsor, together with the Dean.

2 The Bishop of Winchester is still Prelate of the Order, even though Windsor itself is now in the Diocese of Oxford.

3 The symbolic meaning of the Garter was that it represented the unity of the valiant knights who were joined together in honour of knightly virtue. Either from the beginning or not long after, the knight-elect at his vesting ceremony was thus admonished by the Sovereign:

'Tie about thy leg for thy renown this noble Garter, wear it as the symbol of the most illustrious Order, never to be forgotten or laid aside, that thereby thou mayest be admonished to be courageous, and, having undertaken a just war ... that thou mayest stand firm and valiantly and successfully conquer.' (*A Dictionary of Chivalry*—Grant Uden).

4 Since the second world war levée, or full-dress uniform, has not been worn under the mantle of Garter or Thistle knights, or under the mantles of Knights Grand Cross of any other order. Instead, morning dress or service uniform has taken the place of the old under-dress. As a temporary post-war concession when chapters of the orders were resumed, this was reasonable

enough, but it seems a great pity that, after all these years, levée dress or the under-dress peculiar to the Order of the Bath, last seen at a chapter held by George V in 1935, has not been restored. In the case of the Garter, a good case could be made for the retention of an under-dress to include knee-breeches and silk stockings on the grounds that a garter clasped round a trouser leg merely looks ridiculous.

5   Or in the rare event of a disgraced knight being expelled from the order. In the 1914-1918 war, pressure of public opinion was to result in the removal of the banner of the German Emperor, who was an honorary member of the order.

6   Froissart is following the medieval theory which held that the prince could not call himself 'King' until the sacred rites of coronation had taken place. Before he became king, Henry was Duke of Lancaster, inheriting from his father, John of Gaunt.

7   The 'white lace' referred to has found its way into the regalia of other orders of chivalry, notably the Garter and the Thistle, as shoulder knots of white taffeta or silk ribbon. These knots are often referred to as 'Shoulder Knots of the Bath'.

8   Quote from *The Armorial,* vol 4, no 4, July 1964.

Notes to Chapter 6

1   The sheriffs continued to hold office for London and Middlesex until the end of the nineteenth century.

2   When the boy King Edward V, accompanied by his uncle, Richard, Duke of Gloucester, the future King Richard III, arrived in his capital he was greeted by the Lord Mayor and the City fathers (aldermen) in scarlet trimmed with fur, while behind followed five hundred of the most eminent burgesses (liverymen?) in violet gowns. This was in May 1483.

3   Provincial sheriffs of the English counties do not wear robes, but either a modified uniform or court dress with cocked hat.

SHORT BIBLIOGRAPHY

Ashmole, E. . . . . *History of Order of the Garter*
Encyclopaedia Britannica (various vols)
History Today (various vols)
Beltz & Nicolas . . . *History of Knighthood*
Bryant, A. . . . . *The Age of Chivalry*
City of London Ceremonial Book
MS records (Guildhall Library)
Derrington, J. . . . *The Pageant of the Law*
Ede & Ravenscroft . . *Judges' Robing List*
Garner, F. G. & J. F. . . . *Civic Ceremonial*
Cambridge Medieval History (various vols)
Oxford History of England (various vols)
Hargreaves-Mawdsley, W. N. *History of Legal Dress in Europe*
Kendall, P. M. . . . *King Richard the Third*
Myers, A. R. . . . . *England in the Late Middle Ages*
Nicholson, H. . . . *Monarchy*
Ogg, K. A. . . . . *English Government and Politics*
Calendar of State Trials
Boutell's Heraldry
Pine, L. G. . . . . *History of the House of Lords*
The Story of Titles
Schramm, P. E. . . . *History of the English Coronation*
Trevelyan, G. M. . . . *History of England & English Social History*
Uden, G. . . . . *Dictionary of Chivalry*
Wagner, A. . . . . *History of the English Heralds*
Introduction of Peers in House of Lords
Wickham-Legg, L. G. . . *English Coronation Records*

Authorities personally consulted

Sir Anthony Wagner, KCVO, Garter King of Arms
Major General P. B. Gillett, CB, OBE (Secretary of Central Chancery of
    Orders of Knighthood)
The Deputy Governor, HM Tower of London (Col. W. E. Saunders)
The Duke of Norfolk's Secretary, Arundel Castle
The Deputy Librarian of the Guildhall Library, City of London
Sir George Lloyd Jacob, Senior Judge of Chancery Division
Sir Harry Fisher (formerly Chairman of The Bar Council)
The Very Reverend the Dean of Westminster (Dr Eric Abbott)
Messrs Ede & Ravenscroft, Chancery Lane, London, EC

INDEX